MW00466246

The Death of Weinberg:
Poems and Stories

The Death of Weinberg:
Poems and Stories

by

Walter Weinschenk

© 2023 Walter Weinschenk. All rights reserved.
This material may not be reproduced in any form, published,
reprinted, recorded, performed, broadcast,
rewritten or redistributed without
the explicit permission of Walter Weinschenk.
All such actions are strictly prohibited by law.

Cover design by Shay Culligan
Cover image by Cottonbro through Pexels

ISBN: 978-1-63980-258-6

Kelsay Books
502 South 1040 East, A-119
American Fork, Utah 84003
Kelsaybooks.com

*This book is dedicated to my wife, Terri,
and my children, Sam and Rose,
wonderful beyond belief.*

Acknowledgments

I am grateful to the editors of journals in which many of the stories and poems contained herein first appeared:

A Rose for Lana: "Creation"
The Banyan Review: "Sister Speaks with God"
Beyond Words: "The River"
The Bluebird Word: "My Eyes Are Small"
Button Eye Review: "I Come and Go"
Cathexis Northwest Press: "Whatever Might Be There"
The Closed Eye Open: "Beyond"
The Courtship of Winds: "The Death of Weinberg"
The Dillydoun Review: "Shadows"
East by Northeast Literary Magazine: "What I May Become"
The Elevation Review: "Chrysanthemums"
Fauxmoir: "Steamship"
Flumes: "Lighthouse"
The Gateway Review: "The Secret of the Moon"
Grey Sparrow Journal: "Today"
Griffel: "The Desert"
Hare's Paw Literary Journal: "Assateague"
High Shelf: "Headstones"
Lighthouse Weekly: "Underwater"
Lunch Ticket: "Time in Mind," "I Saw a Mountain"
Penumbra: "My Old Dog"
Phantom Kangaroo: "I Was Very Old That Day"
Ponder Review: "Tell Me"
Rat 'n' Rooster Journal of Speculative Fiction and Poetry:
    "Waiting for a Train"
The Raven Review: "The Wagon"
The Raw Art Review: "Deep into the Night"
Sand Hills Literary Magazine: "Fences"
Sheepshead Review: "I Met a King"
Sunspot Literary Journal: "If I Were a Fish"
The Write Launch: "The Garden of Eden"
The Writing Disorder: "Matters That Concern Me"

Contents

Short story titles are noted in bold.

Underwater

I.

I tumbled through
A school of fish,
A swirling horde,
A silver coil
That danced
Around me
Like a circle of light
While, below,
Green lobsters
Trudged along,
Wary and deliberate;
Storms of seaweed
Fell like snow
And gathered in piles;
I saw, as well,
The bones of fish
And the bones of men;
They roll like tumbleweed
Across the floor;
I mourned the loss
Of those nameless souls.

II.

The sun is weak:
Its blinding light
Succumbs to the water,
Gleams meekly
Through shadows
That pervade the ocean's
Rooms and corridors

But, even so,
I now can see
As never before:
I see the flicker
Of distant fins
And grains of sand
In every inch
Of the seabed's
Grand mosaic;
I see sharp corners
And subtle bends
Hidden in a shadow's edge,
And I see colors
That can't be seen
In the atmosphere;
I have found clarity
In the darkness of the sea.

The weight of water
Is soft against my skin:
The cool of it
Reaches my core,
Runs throughout
The essence of all I am,
An essence I never knew
And could never know
Living life on land.

I hear the song
Of bells in the distance;
A strained echo
Reverberates in long,
Deformed tone,
Chimes from beyond the reef;

It could be the music
Of an ancient buoy,
Long ago abandoned
Or, perhaps, the song
Of currents as they cross:
Sober tone,
Holy melody,
A lonely reminder
Of something lost;
The crabs and eels
And angelfish
Listen and live
In keeping
With its rhythm
As I drift, spellbound,
Toward the sound
Of that lament.

The Desert

I left home,
I drove and drove
Beyond the town
Through desert dry;
A man was walking
By the road
As I went speeding by;
I waved my hand
And he waved back;
The moment passed,
And he was gone.

The wind blew cold;
The car slowed down,
Slower, slower, then it stopped;
I got out and began to walk;
The sun drowned
In the sand ahead
And the moon drew up
Like an albatross,
Pale against the sky;
Silver stars across the night,
A thousand at a time.

I walked into the night
And a car came speeding by;
The driver waved and I waved back,
The moment passed and he was gone.

I'm tired and my feet are numb;
The sand has turned to ice;
I have walked a thousand miles,
But I'll walk forever, if I must:

You won't wake up if you stop to rest
On a frozen road in the middle
Of a cruel and bitter desert night.

I Was Very Old That Day

I was very old that day;
Edgy I was, quite afraid
As I lay supine upon the beach,
My mind inverted like a sunken ship,
My arms, my legs, as still as ice
Absorbing heat as best I could
But then I remembered
An array of things
That I'd allowed to languish:
Things quite genuine,
Housed within my head
Yet scattered like toys
In the yard outside;
Things that live and die
Of their own accord:
Someone sitting in a chair,
Swirling curls of silver hair
Asleep upon her shoulder;
Porchlight on a rainy night,
Crayon yellow in the dark,
Crazy moths in senseless circles;
People in the back-and-forth:
Reliable, rapacious,
Loving, loved and leery-eyed;
Winsome moon fading fast,
Lost in morning's winding sheet;
Arms that reach, hands that hold;
Tremble tears and heartache eyes
And then I remembered the so many times
I stepped into the living room
And I could see, as often as not,
A sprawling candelabra
Set upon a white credenza;

Winding silver arms
With upturned palms,
A candle rising out of each,
Dancing veils of yellow light
Like hooded priests in waiting.

If I Were a Fish

If I were a fish (and it may yet come to pass),
I would consign my soul to the water
And wear it like a linen shroud
That moves with me in cool continuum.

I would split the water with my lip
And, with my tail, I'd sew it up;
I'd venture forth as I see fit,
Silver in the morning,
Bloody gold at night.

But never would I break the plane
Of the silver ceiling overhead
(Unless, of course, a fly flew by,
Low enough to snap it up).

For if I were to pierce that mirrored veil
For more than just a moment,
I simply couldn't bear to see
A world that wasn't meant for me,
A world too cruel for piscine eyes:
I'd be overcome by the sorry sight,
Upon the shore, of elderly trees
Enslaved by wind, made to dance,
Their limbs pulled back and snapped
Like whips, and I'd see, as well,
The desperate flight of fathers and mothers
Along the beach, screaming names
Of sons and daughters,
Plucking up children on the run
Before the rains arrive.

The Dusty Old Moon

Poor dusty moon,
Stuck in a rut;
He circles the earth
And cannot stop;
He races along a
Well-worn path.

His orbit is premised
Upon complex laws
That govern space and time,
And there are seismographs
And other tools
To help us understand
His habits and proclivities.

But the matter of the moon
Is simpler than you think:
I know this because
I know the moon;
I know the essence
Of who he is
And I can perceive
His state of mind
By simply looking up
And waving my hand;
He may wink,
Or nod
Or shut his eyes
But if he pretends
Not to notice me,
I can thereby sense
The depth of his unhappiness.

His pale cheeks,
Once smooth with hope,
Are forever marked:
Craters desecrate the beaches
Of unrequited love that run
Across his brow,
And fallow fields of loneliness
Proliferate with each passing day
So that now his face
Is cracked and chipped
Like an old statue,
Left to crumble
In the winter rain.

I don't need a telescope
To know the moon;
I study the pace
Of his evening ascent
To fathom the degree
Of his despondency;
I see the moon for all he is:
A wistful soul
In the cold autumn sky.

I know how he feels
All too well:
I am stuck
In a winding circle
Of my own though,
Of course, my rutted path
Is utterly terrestrial.

Today

No beauty to be found along these wicked streets. I was mildly desperate and had been so for so many years. "What is your purpose?" I asked myself, dizzy with need, not knowing what I needed. Pointless to live through the day just to get to the next, so it seemed to me. *Time to go* is what I thought. I walked to the pier and dove right off and quickly lost sight of the thin grey line.

Seething waves in rhythmic riot: they tried to shake off a flat green patina. I sank fast but, suddenly, everything made sense to me. I was now a citizen of the underneath, the world that no one knows. I laughed when I saw the King, trident held high, as he mingled with the tigerfish jacketed in scales of silver and gold. They shook their fins to show me the way and ushered me over with tails in a flutter. The water was cool but it wasn't cold. There was no worry, no human thing but there were rows of sea anemone, dressed in red, and long green weeds that glided along. It was delightful, I must say. "Today, down here, is quite endless," said the King as I floated by, headed toward a deep ravine. You could say it is forever here and you might not be wrong: no one needs and nothing is needed. I didn't ever want to leave which is why, today, I drift through the shifting depths. I take my rest on the sandy floor where urchins live and crabs wander in ceaseless circles. The sea breathes for me in long draughts. I let the current carry me out through long shafts of angled light.

The Clouds

The clouds were light and wispy edged
And upon a field,
As wide as any field can be,
The women drank and staggered
And then they sat;
They stared overhead, tipsy-eyed
And I could hear them sing:
The clouds are rolling by . . .

The clouds were light and wispy edged
And upon a field,
As wide as any field can be,
The men drank and staggered
And then they sat;
They stared overhead, tipsy-eyed
And I could hear them sing:
The clouds are rolling by . . .

Upon a field
As wide as any field can be
The children ran in circles,
Staggered, laughed
And rolled in the grass
Down the velvet hill
And I could hear them sing:
The clouds are rolling by . . .

I Met a King

Alone upon a country road,
He staggered as he walked;
Torn rags and tangled hair,
Leather skin, silver beard.

He wore a crown of twig and leaf;
His scepter was a willow branch;
A signet ring, thistle and vine,
Was tied around his finger.

I lifted him up and carried him
Like a stack of wood upon my back
But soon I was exhausted;
I set him down and then he spoke:

I rule the sparrows and the crows;
My throne is made of rock;
My army is a pack of wolves;
My land goes on forever.

I have an ocean that has no tide;
I have a road that never ends;
I roam a desert that has no name;
I tend a field of tangled weed.

I see a sun that never sets;
I see a moon that never moves;
I see a sky that withers with age;
I see stars that can't be seen.

I sit by a river that doesn't run;
I stand by a tree that doesn't grow;
I know a god that doesn't know;
I know things I never knew.

I felt his words resound in my heart
But, in my heart, I saw him die;
I bowed but as I stepped away
I fell into his ancient eyes
And realized I could never leave;
The trees leaned in and, as I spoke,
Bore witness to my words:

I will cross a desert that has no name;
I will stare at a moon that never moves;
I will gaze at a sun that never sets;
I will see stars that can't be seen.

I will live in a cave at the edge of the wood;
I will feed on weed and roasted bark;
My beard will fall below my chin;
My hair will lie across my back.

I will rest and I will rise
And I will search for hopeless souls
Lost upon a country road;
I will carry them upon my back
And I will bring them home.

I will rule the sparrows and crows;
I will wear a crown of weeds;
I will wield a willow branch;
I will sleep on a bed of stone;
I will sit upon a rock
And it shall be my throne.

The Wagon

The wagon in which I ride
Slows, stops, mired in mud;
The paint fades beneath the rays
Of an apoplectic sun;
The axle breaks, the wheels fall off,
It crumbles to the ground.

Nighttime has descended,
I don't know where I am,
But I remember a ride I took
And I remember getting out:
I stood alone upon a road;
I saw a light and began to walk.

Chrysanthemums

I am gone,
A memory,
A broken beam of light,
Diffuse in time,
A fading afterthought
But, even so,
A part of me
Still lives:
A silent remnant
That can't be seen;
It roams the earth,
Rises through the silver sheen
Of jeweled spring nights,
Races through clover
And grassy thickets,
Flies like leaves,
Falls from the sky
Like grey rain,
Lands in a twist
And floats again,
Swirls in the breeze
And surfs the wind;
This is how it is
And always will be;
No one knows,
No one sees
But, strange to say,
I am still alive
In the hearts and minds
Of chrysanthemums
Over which I fly;
Living seas of chrysanthemums,
Thick across the fields,
Grand nations, yellow and red;

They call my name,
They sing,
They comfort me
As I pass by,
Each and every time
And this is what
They say to me:

It's warm today,
Quite perfect,
And the breeze is right;
The earth is moist,
It soothes our roots;
We don't know who we are
But we love the day,
Embrace the night;
We breathe and love
And love each breath;
Nurtured, cossetted,
By earth and air;
We are alive
And life itself
Surges through
Our stems and veins;
We stretch our leaves
And gentle petals
Of our floret coats;
We dance in the rain,
We salute the sun;
We stir, we turn
In the world in which
We find ourselves,
Some world, this world
And you as well,

You who are in the world,
One in the world,
Like each of us.

I can't reply
But they know me well,
Better than I know myself;
They tip their petals
On sunny days as I fly by,
Each and every time.

The Death of Weinberg

It astounds me still: the empty, insidious way in which death supersedes the life it devours. But this is old news, too sophomoric to dwell upon and yet I feel the need to mention it because I can't stop thinking about it. It overwhelms me, all of it, perhaps in a different way than once it did but, regardless, my mind relentlessly veers in this direction ever since Weinberg died and I just don't have the wherewithal to alter the course of my thoughts. A man dies, his death is noted, he is mourned, he is mythologized and forgotten. Simply stated, his death overtakes him. It is left to a sorry band of survivors to make sense of it, find order in it, cull meaning out of it and celebrate the premise and theme of that lost life.

But we may not be up to the task. We may not be strong or interested enough to take on the burden and, in fact, we may be too disabled by the passing itself to engage in the aftermath. We may be just strong enough to usher the dead man to the cemetery, rush from the gravesite and confine ourselves to a cell of our own making. We vow to reside there, isolated, shocked, sad, absorbed and silent. We may hide behind the curtain, engage in the fantasy of undoing that which is irrevocable, whisper, cry, look down, look up and fix our gaze upon some crack in the wall that stares at us until, finally, after fruitless attempts to understand the unfathomable, we begin to reacquire our consciousness and begin to see some meaning apparent in the decedent's life, something to latch onto, something we can carry with us. We may, for example, rejoice in his constancy or, perhaps, applaud his flight from constancy but, in any event, we may feel within us disparate pieces of his character coalesce. In that way, we may experience him once more albeit from a different vantage point, feel his presence and discover, perhaps, parallel beauty in lives of our own. When we arrive at that point and that jewel, that medallion, that life is unearthed and set upon the mantle, we polish it with vigor and devotion. We see to it that it shines until it scintillates with the meaning of the man and we keep at it for years through the course of one or two or many generations. Ultimately, however, our collective commitment wanes. The veneer fails, the jewel tarnishes, cracks emerge, fissures deepen and, in the aftermath of death, the decedent dies a second time. It is sad but unavoidable, a painful reality, tragic and draining. Time passes and life goes on. For those who hardly knew him, his death is of no consequence and is, perhaps, a distraction. But I know this: death endows every man with a particular form of dignity and reveals, in most cases, a connection, perhaps imperfect but real, through which he touched others at some point, in some way. Each of us affects another, however oblique or subtle our touch may be. We mourn the dead and, in time, we are remembered. Death breaks hearts and there are thousands strewn about the graveyard: they scatter like leaves in the wind, gather against headstones or align themselves in a sad path that leads from a dead man's plot to your front door. He died, she died and his death and her death envelope us: each death chokes us like some nebulous holy ligature and stings us like the cold air that blows across the pier upon which we stand while azure breakers, capped white, swell and roll senseless in front of us. It is cold now and you are freezing. All that you want right now and all that you will ever want, or so you believe, is to be warm again. Standing at the gravesite or sitting at your desk, in the heat of summer or prison of winter, you stare at his picture or imagine his image and realize in a sudden that you are cold. You feel the need to reach for a sweater that isn't there. You would happily grab that sweater, any sweater, if you were lucky enough to find it hanging from a doorknob or hanger and you wouldn't care in the least how old it is or the style of it or the size of it. You would gratefully accept it whether tattered or intact, whether heavy with threads of wool or threadbare. Death has brushed up against you and you silently vow that if you were somehow granted a single wish by some providential power, you would plead for warmth and, were you to find it, you would be forever grateful and assuaged. And if that sweater were to fall from an angel's lair high above the earth straight into your outstretched arms, you would be saved: you would frantically thrust your head through the top of it and push your arms through its sleeves and you would be set, all will have been made right, at least for the moment. You would feel the comfort of your body's warmth trapped within its channels and occlusions: the heat of it would collect and recirculate in and around your freezing skin and your arms would absorb that heat as if they had long been thirsty for it and, yes, you will have been delivered, heaven will have clothed you in a bulwark that will shield you from death's malignant air. And days or months or years later, while walking along the road or, while seated at the kitchen table, suddenly, without warning, you will feel the onslaught of that same despicable cold as it claims your skin once more, relentless and unmoved by your protests and the tremulations of your shivering body. Someday, no doubt, you will find yourself, once again, unbearably cold. The matter will take on urgency and you will twist in its grasp and silently scream in desperation, driven by the force of its cruelty and you will realize, at that moment, that the only thing that stands between your life and the end of it is a simple woolen sweater, red, grey, old, new, it makes no difference: you will be saved if only it were to fall into your outstretched arms. When these moments come (and they undoubtedly will arrive) you will stand, then as now, in cold despondency. Of course, this form of suffering comes without warning as when, for example, one of the law firm partners calls and stammers in slow and confidential tone as if providing a stock tip: "Did you hear . . . about Weinberg . . . he died . . . Weinberg died on Tuesday," and it is now Thursday and, having just learned that your partner, Weinberg, has died, you sit at the table, startled, unsure, unnerved for a long moment. It takes a few seconds for you to react, to get back to who you are or, rather, who you thought you were prior to the news of Weinberg's demise. But you snap back, you proceed forth in the very same manner in which you undertake projects and formulate responses: you seek information, you ask about funeral arrangements, you wonder aloud about shiva, you consider the suit you typically wear to funerals and you ask how long the decedent suffered. In the course of your inquiry, you are suddenly thrown off-kilter: you remember your own prior commitments and you are disturbed. An image of your day planner takes form in your consciousness and, at this juncture, you begin the process of prioritizing business calls and scripting appropriate replies to rely upon when rescheduling your appointments. You are sad, you had known Weinberg forever, you had worked with him for years but, if truth be told, you weren't overly fond of him. You enjoyed his company on most days but he was a horror when things didn't go his way. He was a good lawyer, charismatic, a real rainmaker but was often loud, self-consumed and abrasive. He would talk incessantly about his cases and drone on about subjects that interested only him and an arrogant smile would erupt upon his face when it was apparent that he was well versed in matters of which you were ignorant. He could be witty and interesting but, in truth, you couldn't say he was a friend.

In the days that follow his death, you begin to resent his imposition upon your time and upon your life. You feel anger, though tempered, at the sudden necessity to rearrange your priorities but, intertwined in the jumble of your thoughts and feelings, an unadulterated sadness rises out of your depths and rushes through your core like hot exhaust from a jet engine. You are confounded by the fact that Weinberg was alive on Monday, died on Tuesday and it is already Thursday and it shocks you that Weinberg, the Weinberg you know, has been dead for two days during which time you went about the vagaries and minor dramas of your life. Now, in a sudden, you miss him, you wish to see him, you want to invite him to lunch, you want to apologize for liking him less than you could have and you begin to feel a hurt of the sort that you felt when you first learned that your father died: it stung then and it stings now, it throbs like a toothache, it unfurls itself like an ill-defined bruise upon your skin, it stares at you in random and unjust ways, it speaks to you in the private language of your own old hurt and you feel the callous inequity and permanence of it. It feels oddly similar though not as deep or cutting as the way it felt so long ago. You feel defrauded, victimized, robbed of some valuable, necessary thing. Weinberg was a fixture of sorts, everyone knew him, everyone wound up liking him despite the coarseness of his nature and he knew everyone you know and he was a part of the collective life in which you are invested and now, suddenly, he isn't alive. Weinberg shouldn't have died and people like him shouldn't die and memories of Weinberg come to you in in bits and flashes and you are now cold, very cold, and you long for warmth and you wait for it in vain.

For those who outlive the decedent, the aftermath of a man's life is the flux in which we swim. It flows forth, it overcomes us and subsumes us. It is a psychic body bag in which we wrestle but are unable to claw our way out. And it is the aftermath, not the death of the man, that is the problem for me, at least at this particular moment. Weinberg's death is a fait accompli, but the long, tedious aftermath of his life has just begun. I am frozen within it, I am but a component in the massive, wide glacier that comprises it as it inches forward imperceptibly, oblivious to the demands of human time. This glacier doesn't know or care about me. It is a construct premised upon ancient human formulations and protocols that never vary but thread through the fabric of life and the rise and demise of untold generations: it is ignorant of our daily struggles and is unmoved by the weight of obligation that the living must bear. It stands aloof and refuses to acknowledge my various needs which are abundant: I need to arrange a funeral, I need to write an obituary, I need to find Weinberg's will and I need to open an estate. The aftermath of Weinberg's life is blind to the urgency of my plight and ignores the fact that I have Weinberg's myriad clients, all strangers, to reassure and I have hundreds of files to review, judges and

35

lawyers to inform, accounts to settle, a safety deposit box to open and examine, a key to locate in order to unlock that box, papers to sort through, court appearances to cover, a trove of additional bills to pay and a thousand phone calls to make. I thought of the way in which our law firm letterhead would need to be updated and my heart sank at the realization that this was but the first drop in a sea of tasks, details, obligations, filings, letters, forms, claims, appointments and projects to which I would now need to attend and oversee. Some of these tasks would be daunting and some would be routine but, collectively, they would be exasperating and time consuming. It would begin with letterhead and would multiply exponentially with each passing hour. Somehow, I had been chosen to sort it all out and I had been made accountable on his behalf. What transpired is that I had become his sole and permanent pallbearer: I carry Weinberg upon my back, long after he left us, through the aftermath of his life. I am one with it and I am driven by it and dragged along with it and I am overcome by the weight and extent of it. It is an edifice in itself and, at this juncture, I remain unsure of its length and depth. It takes wide turns and I'm not sure how wide those turns may turn out to be but I understand, quite clearly, that its substance and direction are rooted in him, in his time, in his history and character. It reaches back to the moment he entered the world and has traveled with him ever since. It meanders through his relationships and his victories and disputes and losses and it ambles along the streets he crossed and inhabits the homes in which he lived and the towns through which he passed. It runs through his disappointments, his accomplishments, his fears and ambitions, his demands, his fits of anger and spasms of jealousy and it lingers in his pettiness and it permeates the array of minor resentments he collected. It rises out of his generosity and it rides the back of his sense of humor. The trail of it reaches back through law school and runs forward through the course of his marriage and the saga of his divorce and the intricate latticework of his broken promises and it lurches from one altercation to the next. It finds him consumed with pity and compassion for the vulnerable, despondent people he represented. It follows him through the corridors of the courthouse and his countless entries and exits through our own office door. It drifts through languid clouds of cigarette smoke that perpetually hung from his office ceiling and it seeps into the floorboards. It underlies the words he read in law books, newspapers and treatises and it settles in the dust that collected upon his tattered sofa and old chairs. It is caught in the frames that embraced faded paintings that hung askew from his walls and it is ground into the worn carpet. It runs through the dank corners of our suite of offices, across aged papers and unanswered letters and unpaid bills and old law books that have sat for years upon chairs intended for the convenience of clients. It runs along the electric cord that connected his old coffee maker to the wall. And it saturates the words he spoke, words I heard, words that can never again be spoken or heard, words borne of an adroit mind, confident words, understandable words, meaningful words, words quoted from his memory of old cases, stories, jokes, intimate depictions of old judges and remembrances of cases won and rueful accounts of cases he wished he had won, theories comprised of brilliant words, wonderful in their simplicity, words of advice directed toward me in careful cadence, keen assessments of fact and law and risk, warm words, kind words, spirited words, gruff words, all said and now done. The life in him streams toward me through his kind bright eyes and runs like tears across his puffy cheeks and creased jowls and falls upon his heavy arms and torso. It runs through his silver hair and the back of his pink neck and across broad shoulders. It lingers over mottled skin and rings the finger that he would raise to the ceiling to emphasize a point. It clings to his arms as they fall and slap in unison upon his thighs as a way to punctuate a story and it loops around his wide throat, rises with his voice that rings in our ears as he launched laughter that leapt high across bookshelves and into the ceiling. It reveals itself in the open embrace of his empathetic, kind heart. This

37

was, and is, his aftermath. It has a life of its own and it radiates in all directions.

In the initial days that followed his death, I didn't quite know what to do. My mind was unsettled and my thoughts were warped like beams of light that gravity bends around the waist of a massive planet. I attended his funeral and I offered a eulogy and, through the course of my tribute, I felt miserably cold.

It is only recently that I have begun to collect my bearings but I see what lies ahead. I have a sense of my mission which will, undoubtedly, go on for quite some time. I realize, however, that it will someday end: the aftermath of Weinberg's life, as immeasurable as it now seems, will itself die in the course of time. Its waves will subside, its currents will ebb and, eventually, its ripples will lap the shore and seep into the sand. And when my death comes, the word will spread, perhaps slowly, perhaps quietly. In response to the few who inquire, others may answer: "He was a lawyer, he worked with Weinberg."

Lighthouse

I was lost but then, by chance,
I found the beach; I walked upon
The scrabble sand; I climbed the rocks
And knew that I would never leave.

I found the lighthouse by the shore;
I climbed the tower to the top;
I lit the lamp and scanned the sea
In search of lost and scattered souls.

The sky was black and ruthless;
My heart broke for the thought
Of sailors trapped in broken boats,
Their draughts of hope consumed.

It was, indeed, a powerful light:
Stately beam, rhythmic reach,
Back and forth like a metronome
And out of darkness souls emerged
Like pearls upon a velvet sleeve:
In perfect line, they sailed toward me.

A shattered armada drifted in,
Staggered toward the shore;
Ripped sails and broken masts;
Their figureheads had lost their heads.

I am no god, a shepherd at best
But it doesn't matter who I am,
For I will climb those steps again
And every night I will shine a light
To bring those children home.

Sister Speaks with God

from Elegy for Sister

Sister says that she spoke with God
Who spoke to her in whitewater flood,
Words in a torrent, God's holy voice
Came to sister in the course of a dream.

That answer was long overdue:
Years of prayer and desperation,
Entreaties carefully crafted, aimed
In careful angle toward the beige baked sky,
Launched like messages in bottles
That float slow vulnerable
And then turn back, return to shore,
Captive to the laughing tide.

Resolute sister prayed and waited,
Allowed her words to float
Until they broke, at last,
Beyond the waves and swells
That, on other days,
Would have pushed them back
Toward the long beach of her consciousness.

Clearly, God could not pretend
That sister's words could not be heard
Or had failed to echo within the space
That separates the holy from the flawed;
Her words, in fact, resounded
Within the holy sanctum.

God listened to her prayer
(Simple, plaintive supplication)
And, this time, answered her

In perfect words that fell to earth;
But sister had retreated,
Found refuge in a thicket:
A vestibule that she believed
Was far beyond harm's reach;
She lay tangled peaceful in the weeds,
Fell asleep and wouldn't wake up,
Supine beneath the senile trees;
Branches out like outstretched arms
Held vigil over her.

As the sky rolled by,
God's words fell loud like rain
Between the twisted fingers
Of those ancient branches;
Sister heard what she had waited for
And opened her eyes:
Myriad holy words in piles
Lay strewn upon the ground;
She picked them up
And wore those words upon her head,
A crown of twigs and red edged leaves.

The Weeds

Big noise in the garden that day,
All that clambering:
Flowers heed the unspoken summons,
Rise warm in maniacal mission;
Primrose, daffodil,
Snowdrop, crocus
And some too green to figure out
But fragile in the air;
They crowd the field,
Reaching up for dear existence;
Can't be rushed but can't be stopped;
They stretch to the sky as if called upon,
Frenetic and fanatic.

Twists, shoots;
Reddish hue,
Big leafy tufted,
Wide upon the ground
And spears of leaves,
All rolled up,
Longing to explode;
Thistle and bud,
Flat-winged leaves like open palms
And light green sheaf-like arrow wings;
Petals combed with streaks of blue,
Red and orange, yellow too,
Like suits and gowns
In a fitting room.

The edifice rises up from under,
Founders in the ground at first
Between the thick black clods;
Roots tangle and drown
In sin and water,

But the mass arises eventually
And all those tiny buds and shoots
Are overcome with joy and mistiness
Like salve across the soft green flesh,
Driven by intelligence of a different sort:
They leap deranged toward the sky;
Hopeful dissonance,
The noise of life erupting.

The sky overhead
Was pale that day,
Blanched but somewhat beige,
Too weak to keep the rain from falling
And, in the yard,
They yearned for air,
They ached for water
And craved life itself
As if it were a meal
And, in fact,
The rains came down
Like the onset of hope
Among the stems
And you could hear
The soft thorns singing;
A waking song,
An overture of grand design,
A melody of purpose;
You could feel it, unexpurgated;
Those flowers dangled like chandeliers
And thin green arms stretched out
Toward the cream ball sun
As if the sun were some maestro,
A mastermind who leads you through
A symphony of seasons;

Raindrops like notes upon the ground;
You couldn't help but hear that song
While passing through the garden.

Stems and barrels,
Hollow tubal joists
Give form
To the living monolith,
A city of a sort
In the act of waking up,
Nudged awake
By primordial restlessness,
An ancient yearning;
It seeps into the tissue
And flows through living,
Breathing channels
Of the hibernating mind;
Pale capillaries
And old consciousness,
Echoes of an ageless song
Implicit in the quiver
Of tiny fibers
Across nubile leaves
And all along the edges;
An awkward reminder
Of mortality,
Presently ignored:
Those leaves
Will be the first to freeze
When the seasons pass
And the cold winds come.

But what about the weeds?
Some stand alone

And bide their time
But most of the weeds are otherwise:
The garden is replete
With weedy vines;
They slink like snakes
Without a sound
Across the yard
And then they climb;
They are the murderous kind;
They engage in quiet violence
As if it were an art;
Pure disdain for anyone
Who dares to breathe;
Curled and primed,
They crawl stealthily
Along the ground,
Entangle themselves
Among stems and stalks;
Tie and tighten like ligature
Until the victim suffocates;
Cruel constrictors,
Lustful and seditious.

They are filled with animus
But self-hate is the driver:
They hate themselves
Because they are alive
And suffer the guilt
Implicit in existence;
They reel beneath that weight
But their hate lies hidden,
Even from themselves;
It lives somewhere beneath
Their consciousness;

Cynical apostles,
Faithful only to themselves,
They maintain their fatal vow
And rampage chaotic
Until, one day,
The cold air comes
And they relent,
Lie dormant for the winter
Stretched across the yard.

They lurked and plotted
Like the killers they are
As I passed by,
But murder doesn't fill the void;
They are empty
And empty they shall always be;
They clamber about
But in a different way;
Cruel and criminal manifestation
Of a private struggle:
Intimations of despair,
A quiet, ruthless kind.

Walking Home, Late Afternoon

Something troubles you this afternoon:
Something that you can't define;
It bothered you yesterday
And waits for you tomorrow;
A rash across your consciousness;
The sky so clear, the air so still;
But there it is, always there,
Even as you walk.

You sleep in its deep embrace
And now it calls from afar
With a voice that is yours;
Distant, aloof but lurks within;
Hard to tell, as time goes on,
How much of it is really you.

Some strange haze
Through which you crawl
Drifts though you as well;
It boils in the cauldron
Of your solitary self
And, all the while,
It holds you in its loving arms.

Nameless jailer, you know him well:
He is you within yourself
Through the million moments of your life;
He is your thinking, dreaming self;
Consumes you while you're standing still;
Becomes you while you're walking home,
All alone, in the afternoon.

Matters That Concern Me

I've experienced some difficulties lately. I'm thinking of the most recent chapter of my life though that chapter may not be as recent as I suppose it to be. Hard to say, hard to think. I'm speaking of the project I've completed. I have built additional brick walls within the confines of my room to buttress existing walls. I had planned this endeavor for quite some time and designed it with precision and constructed it with care and, presently, the brick reinforcement that I had envisioned and needed in a dire way stands firmly before me. Though it took considerable effort, that effort is best understood as a symptom, a side-effect or manifestation of limitless need, an ever-evolving need that I don't quite understand. It rises and dissipates, hibernates and wakes, sleeps and rouses itself in some part of me and, without hesitation or forethought, proceeds to wage war against me from within. It is an asphyxiation of sorts. The present expression of this come-and-go need, this rise-and-fall desperation is only one chapter in an endless array of chapters in my book of need and is by no means the last chapter or next-to-last chapter. It can be said that the struggle to resolve raw need serves to define me, more or less, and dictates my choices and establishes my proclivities and predominates my life.

In this particular case, I had a need and this particular need could not be ignored and attending to it could not be delayed. The nature of that need, this time, was much in line with the way it always is though somewhat at variance with it. I have added a brick lining to the walls in my room despite the fact that the room was not very large to begin with and isn't simply a room: it is, in a very real sense, a sanctuary, some days more than others. The old walls that defined the room (and there could not have been a room without the presence of those walls) had been in place for as long as I can remember and those walls continue to stand but, somehow, I became convinced that they were not enough. I came to believe that the walls as they existed were in need of immediate fortification and so, now, they are fortified. I was sure that the added strength would provide longevity. There was no other possibility, there was no other way to live, it could be no other way, it had to be just so, now and forever. It's done, at least for now and, perhaps, forever.

It took some time, I forget how much time. It was backbreaking labor though I hardly remember having been engaged in the process. The dull clay lining of brick, the color of overripe fruit, is solid and sublime. The work is complete in every way at this particular juncture. I know it, I see it and I presently experience it but the story of its construction is a dim memory, barely a memory which is, more or less, the equivalent of a dream and, like a dream, it is ephemeral and dissipates in time. A dream cannot be explained and the same holds true for memory: it cannot be explained. I have created a new reality for myself in the form of new brick walls, but I am the only one who sees those walls and appreciates that reality. It is, nevertheless, a statement that I alone could have made and thereby provides absolute proof in my own eyes of my own effort and, no doubt, I had to have made such effort to get to this point and achieve what has been achieved thus far. There is no other explanation. It is there, I am here and my new reality is confirmed by the fact that the area of my room has now been diminished by the area of space committed to, and consumed by, the additional inner wall that now stands flush against the existing wall to which it is adjoined.

The job seems to have been done rather well, at least that's my impression. Those bricks are as straight as straight can be. They run perfectly across and around me as any horizon you might detest with all your heart as you stand upon the beach and peer out in all directions. That horizon is the only thing you see. It encompasses you like a circle of elderly trees. Detest, I say, because that horizon

49

is perfectly straight, sharp against the sky and well-defined in a threatening manner like the edge of a razor that needs to be kept at a distance for fear of the potential that lies within it like electric current that rides within a wire and can't be seen but threatens because it exists and is, in this way, quite inhuman, perfectly inhuman. The vertical lines are plumb, of that you can be sure. What I'm left with is a hardened insular lining. I am protected like a fox in a lair, a bear in a cave, no doubt you understand, you've been there. You might even picture yourself sitting in my room in place of me, needing something, wanting something, faced with a predicament that can never be defined even if you took all the time until the end of time and back to the moment that has just passed to define that need, that predicament, that problem and you might as well spend the whole of your life seeking a resolution that is somehow satisfactory. In fact, it becomes you all at once and you find yourself doing just that, seeking something out, seeking the answer, all the while knowing there is no answer and so you let it go until it arises again. It's a never-ending start and stop. I said that it becomes you and that is unfortunate but, after all, we are only human. It is hard to keep it all in mind because the memory of the problem and solution are crushed, one atop the other, each forged into the other so that each consumes the other, each overtakes the other, each is enmeshed and adjoined with the other in the way that a crimson meteor crashes to earth and becomes one with it so that there is only one thing left. The two become one and one is all that remains and all there is. It is an answer of sorts. The resolution has been formulated and all will be fine, at least for a while, until the problem reemerges years or months or seconds from now and, once more, it will stare you down, mock you, concern you, seek your pity or petition you for closure until you can no longer stand that state of irresolution and you feel compelled to resolve it, once again, knowing that it's not within your power to resolve in any effective, enduring way. For now, however, the new brick wall—my double wall—will suffice. It is a holy bulwark. It will harden until it is no longer capable of hardening and, at some particular time, it will cease to be a memory. I will have become accustomed to it and I will come to believe that there never was a time at which it did not exist.

But it is not fear of a thing that gives rise to the problem and it is not fear of a person that gives rise to the problem because, in truth, there's nothing I seek to avoid and I have no one to fear. The problem is a bit more complex, I suppose. It begins with me: I bask in my own invisibility. I celebrate my own distance from things. I see a world that exists beyond my window and beyond my walls but I need to be decisively separated from it which is why I watch the world through my window which allows me to perceive it and remain far from it. I am here and there, I am in and out, I can see but can't be seen. I feel secure and insecure simultaneously and it is a remarkable thing.

I raise my head slowly so my eyes are positioned just above the sill and I peer out at whomever walks by but their presence is announced long in advance by the shuffling of their footsteps upon the pebbly pavement. I feel each respective presence rise and fade, much like the memories and dreams that invade my consciousness in the moments just before my eyes are scalded open by the light of morning while (and all the while) I remain untouched, unseen, unknown and, in fact, my eyes have their own innate desire to latch on to those who walk by. Passersby approach from the end of the street and cross directly in front of the window through which I stare and I will sit and wait and suddenly, as if on cue, I will see someone, anyone, walking along the sidewalk in my direction. There appears a man, there appears a woman, there appears the postal worker making his or her rounds, there appears the delivery man or the plumber or the electrician or the person who walks for the sake of walking. If I wait long enough, I will have something that resembles an encounter, one in which my eyes are steady above the sill as I peer out and focus upon random people and I watch each of them but none of them perceives the traction of my vision upon their backs, none of them senses the drag of my cognizance of their existence upon their consciousness, none of them feels the great weight of my own existence upon their respective psyches though it seems to me that my stare is so heavy and so immensely forceful that it surprises me that no one feels the trembling mass of it or senses the heat of it or hears the drone of it.

I wind up thinking very hard and wondering very hard. I gaze and speculate, I gaze and wonder, I gaze and fall into an ocean of want, a river of need. I need to know who it is that my eyes follow. I need to know the thoughts that are housed in his or her head. I need to know what lies within the inner sanctum of his or her essential self but I know that it's impossible to know. There is no language through which that self can be communicated. This question, this predicament, can never be resolved. Conversation is inadequate no matter how honest and earnest and open people may be. That is the problem, it's a real problem: it is an unending deficit, a perpetual hiatus, an experiential nausea and it causes me to suffer from one moment to the next and, perhaps, I'm the only one who feels it and faces it and cowers before it.

This is my pattern, this is my purpose, this is my sequence, this is the order and character of events that comprise the ether of my experience and it provides the semblance of a source of meaning that can't be explained but exists and takes the form of an underlying vibration that coops the space within my being. It is an unwanted noise, a throb of consciousness that claims my entire attention as I pace the inner sanctum of my room. It is, perhaps, the wriggling embryo of an enigma that lifts its head and arises unannounced and needs to be resolved and, when it yawns and wakes and pulses, it requires that I attend to it. It is a continuum, a unitary problem that has phases just as you and I experience the flow and confluence of day and night, wakefulness and unconsciousness though each phase has a different feel over time. Consequently, my existence can be summarized as a continuing dialectic, a quivering procession, an unending effort to apply salve to an unending series of lacerations. Problem, resolution, problem, resolution, over and again: it is tantamount to a sweeping, desperate effort to satisfy a craving for refuge within an enclave or behind some rock or curtain or wall. I seek an escape from the eyes of others. I need to remain unseen. I reserve and effectively retain my place outside the line of sight so that others may remain oblivious to my existence while my eyes fill with theirs. I suppose there is nothing new or exciting about this. I'm no different than anyone else. I suppose we occupy ourselves in individual efforts to rectify or resolve whatever requires resolution, each in our own way, though I really wouldn't know, will never know, can never know.

I rarely leave. I stay within my own very well-defined perimeter that is framed by solid physical borders, now bolstered to an even greater degree by the addition of a solid brick lining with a surface so rough and real that it scrapes my skin as I brush my hand against it. Even if I wanted to saunter out on my own in the pale light of day, it would be difficult to do so. Even if I no longer savored the space between myself and others and even if I felt compelled for some reason to link arms with he or she who walks down the street, even if I wished to join the ranks of humanity, even if I felt a need to stand on some street corner and greet each passerby as each passed by and extend my best wishes in the form of joyful words that surge out of me and flow through the medium of my raspy voice, it would be so difficult, so extremely difficult. It is difficult to leave the castle keep within which I have enveloped myself though, of course, I need to emerge every now and then because the exigencies of life demand it. One must shop for groceries, one must buy clothes, one must argue with one's neighbor or stand still upon the stool while the tailor draws the dull chalk like a knife across the coarse fabric of one's new suit and one must sit in the chair while one's hair is styled as pieces of it fall past one's eyes onto the floor and one must complete an array of tasks and indulge in various rituals and seek various allowances to accomplish the entirety of it all, the grand act of living. One needs to leave one's home. If you wish to live, you have no choice but to walk out into the world. But to get out, you must get in and this is no easy feat. First, there is the street and the doorway that would need to be opened, a heavy wood door, modern, pale like the skin of an old apple, beset by a small window that stares out warily like some cyclops eye, too small and high to be of much use to anyone and if that door were a face, it would be the blandest of faces, unknowing and apathetic. Despite its appearance, that door would open easily but only after the latch is released and, unfortunately, it is often a bit difficult to manage. It takes time to jiggle the key so that the latch turns but it becomes a habit after a number of attempts like anything else in life. As you enter you would walk and as you walk you would find that there is a steady lowering of the ceiling that looms over you, high above your head at first but drops steadily at a gradual angle and lowers to such an extent that it almost brushes against your scalp as you pass beneath it and there comes a point at which you are forced to crawl along the floor to get to where you need to be. As you proceed through the corridor, the flat blue matte walls are gradually overtaken by shadow but you navigate through it, narrow as it is, as the heat almost overtakes you and you struggle through two or three twists and turns, much like the jumble of paths and furrows that cross, back and forth, within some labyrinthine hedge maze until you are delivered into the confines of a small anteroom, not much larger than the dimensions of a Kashan rug, floral gray, no larger than a kitchen table, onto which you step and, leaving it behind, you notice (and you will notice) that the room has no prominent features other than a bookshelf and lamp. You notice that these walls, unlike the walls through which you have crawled, are spotted copper much like the sienna spotted skin of your own arms that you can still see in the dim, dull light. You sense the odor of plants and soil and moisture and, indeed, there are several wilting

54

Philodendron set neatly on a narrow table that run the length of the wall in front of you. At this point, you have no choice but to commit to climbing a black steel spiral staircase which you approach by stepping through an open archway. You climb up and around the incremental steps that wind tight like a spring, your hand firm upon the winding rail as you walk in tiny, concentric circles and rise for an indefinite time and it seems like such a long time though you realize, soon, that it is but a moment until you reach the hallway, lit bright by a modest chandelier that protrudes overhead and shows you the way and guides you along but if you could only see the structure through which you have just ascended, you'd know that you've risen through a small white tower, a turret of sorts, which embraces a lone window with curtain drawn. If you were to study this tower from the street, you'd note to yourself that the window is framed in black. That window is my window. You'd notice as well that my tower is topped with a cone roof, a primitive hat built of slate shingles that wind around in circles, smaller and smaller, culminating in a pin-like point at the very top but you are inside, not outside, and you have now come face to face with the cedar door to my room and, if you were to enter, you would notice the brick lining that buttresses my walls and you would see the lone black-framed window with curtain drawn, that same window you noticed while standing on the street and you would see me sitting at my desk or standing by the mirror or lifting the curtain that hangs in the window in order for me to peek out of it and, having arrived, you might not remember how you got there. It may feel like a dream or a memory and, though your journey is vague like a dream or a memory, it is a reality nonetheless. You are now here and being here is proof of the fact that you came here whether or not you remember the details of how it is you arrived.

This is how it is but it's not the entire picture. What's missing are the fields and forests of experience and the tangle of gullies and gorges of thought and need and resolution that come together to

55

form an inextricable knot that comprises the evanescent conundrum that is my essential self. What's missing is the sublime feeling that comes over me as I find my bed at night after having jettisoned many of my preoccupations. I lie down upon a bed that is situated beside and beneath the sill of the window, the window I've described. I lie down and my head is so close to that window that I can feel the chill of its frame in winter and the heat of its pane in summer. I am secure in the knowledge that my window is immediately accessible and it happens to be the case that many of my concerns wash away like leaves in the rush of a river in spring and this sense of peace arises only because I realize that my window is so close at hand. The air settles around me and it is then that I hear the sounds of distant things. I hear the rolling of railroad wheels. I hear the insane drone of motorcycles on a highway. I hear the languid groan of a plane overhead. I hear all these things and, as I hear them, I feel myself drawn like a minnow into a gentle eddy of cool serenity. I revel in the sense of distance between myself and the train and the motorcycle and plane and I can almost imagine the thoughts and concerns of people aboard trains or people who ride motorcycles or people who sit high in flight above the clouds. I delight in the mystery of that distance. It feels as though I can see them though they have no conception of me and have no reason to think of me but I think of them always and can practically visualize the expressions on their faces. I embrace them in my mind but they would have no reason to think of someone who thinks of them, someone who projects a conception of them into his own consciousness and takes pleasure in that distance as he lies in bed on the verge of sleep and, in his final wakeful moments, wonders not of himself but of them. It is an aberration of intimacy. It is an elegy to the tenuous ties that connect me loosely to others as I meander through the shadows of their lives. It is life passing in different directions, one past the other, each and all somehow free and somehow tethered. This is how it is as I stare into the grey-black ceiling above me searching for planes and trains and motorcycles as

56

the darkness of that ceiling becomes my own dark night and my eyelids sink into the floor of the gorges of my eyes like the overhead doors of a warehouse that slowly close at the end of a long day.

This is how it is but it is only part of my particular picture because, like everyone else, I wake up. These matters, these sensations, this procession of thought and the long coil of longing are the remains that I gather. They are part of the whole. The dreams that cascade through the thermosphere of my sleep are forever lost within the whirlwind of my own oblivion except for bits and pieces. What's left are fragments of thought and memories of a dream rather than the thought itself or the dream itself. Dreams fade, memories fade, the sense of things fade, it all fades so incredibly fast. No matter how hard one tries, those dreams and memories and sensations cannot be retrieved but for the edges and corners. A moment or two passes and my thinking mind returns and its quadrants quickly fill with complete thoughts, rigid thoughts, and this barrage of thought is inconsequential though some of these fleeting thoughts are worth hanging onto. There is always a category of thought that is key to survival and must be retained and developed if one is to navigate life and progress or proceed to some destination, however defined. These are the mundane thoughts, the practical thoughts that serve as markers etched onto one's mental compass and, in fact, much of my thinking is devoted to practical things such as cooking but I soon veer from the practical and settle into a quasi-reverie that is a peculiar form of consciousness in itself. These are the moments that I spend wondering and peering out the window during the days that my eyes wish to wander like children.

I cannot know anyone in any real sense but if there is an exception, if there is one person who is capable of being known, it is the blind tenant who lives across the hall. He is remarkable and astonishing but, as extraordinary as he is, I am discouraged in his presence. I may visit him or not but I am less inclined than ever to interact with him and I have purposely kept my interactions with him to a minimum since these encounters always end in a way that is debilitating and unsettling. I do visit him, however, from time to time. I cross the hall, I knock on the door and I hear the latch unlock from within. The door opens wide and the light of another world pours forth over me like shafts of sunrise. Before me stands the blind tenant who ratchets his head down to face me and his face formulates a smile as soon as he hears my voice. He is tall and heavy, his shoulders are wide and his red tussled hair falls unevenly about his neck and ears. He embraces me, he grasps my shoulders, he pulls me through the door, he ushers me around a sparsely furnished room as he begins to talk and he rambles incessantly in a voice that is both gruff and happy and pleasing. He offers beer or bourbon or wine and I take him up on it, I drink with him, I drink the beer or bourbon or wine and I ask for more and he delights in pouring. I drink until I'm drunk, I laugh at his jokes, I listen to his story and he and I join in laughter. He laughs uproariously. We toast each other. We exclaim "to life!" in unison and we continue to drink but, invariably, the visit takes an odd turn. He'll draw me over to the large living room window that overlooks a street that runs parallel to the street that I look out upon. He'll open that window as wide as he can and, as blind as he is, he'll somehow know that someone is just then passing, close upon the sidewalk. Somehow, he will spot that person who is no one in particular. It may be some unsuspecting dog walker, for example, and he'll yell, "Good morning," though it's long past morning. The dogwalker may yell back, "Good morning," and the blind tenant and the dogwalker might then carry on animated conversation about dogs and walking and the winter to come. I can only hear one side of the conversation but I do hear the laughter that comes from each side of the window as that laughter punctuates the give-and-take of their conversation. It is at this juncture that I begin to feel distance between myself and the blind tenant and the space between us explodes in the minefield of my mind and it is at about this time that I decide to leave. Even though their conversation

58

continues and the blind tenant and the dogwalker are happily engaged in explaining themselves and telling tales and recounting the twisting turns of their respective lives, I will feel an overpowering urge to leave, to escape, to run for my life and I will feel aching, debilitating need coalesce within me as though it were organic and ready to ferment or fester like infection. I find my way out. I fall through the door while the blind tenant continues his conversation. I stagger back across the hall, I see my cedar door and I crash into it. I open it quickly and I close it quickly and I throw myself onto my bed and I let the experience come to an inglorious end. I let it become a memory. I let it be what it is: something that I cannot quite grasp, something that evades me. I proceed to let months or weeks or days pass until the time comes, once more, to visit the blind tenant. Though it may be long, long, long into the future, that day invariably comes and, invariably, I summon the will to visit again. I always visit again.

There is more, however. There is more that I encounter, more to my reality and more to the tunnel of experience through which I pass. There is the matter of rent and there is the matter of the landlady. Rent is one of those things that one must deal with. The landlady is real and my obligation to pay rent to her is real. It is the pinion that holds the wheel in place and allows it to spin in circles. There is also the matter of the landlady's daughter who is no longer young but, when she was young, I was young as well. When we were children, the landlady's daughter would run in circles and I would run after her. She had heather hair and her bangs would bounce against her forehead as she ran. She would laugh while she ran and, when she laughed, two glistening front teeth would ride high in her mouth and, indeed, she would laugh quite often. I would laugh as well. There was joy in running and there was joy in laughing and I recall running and falling and laughing. It would not be an exaggeration to say that we were inseparable. On occasion, she and I might sing. We would collect sticks. We would see who could jump the highest or farthest and we would march into piles of leaves with great vehemence. We would strip petals from flowers in the garden. We would dig through the dirt with our fingers. We would retreat to the steps and sit. It may have seemed as though we were waiting for someone to arrive or something to happen but, in fact, we were waiting for nothing and no one at all. Her favorite color was blue and blue became my favorite as well. Sadly, the friendship came to an end when she began having problems with her legs. She had trouble running and then she had trouble walking and there came a time at which she could run or walk no more. She sat in a wheelchair from that point on. I saw less and less of her until I hardly saw her at all.

There is also the matter of the landlady's son who lives somewhere nearby and visits his mother on occasion. I don't know his name though, perhaps, I should. He is thin and his arms dangle as he walks and he wears a fedora and I find him repulsive. He doesn't comport with my conception of what a landlady's son should be. He doesn't fit the model. He is overly confident and self-assured, he is loud, he is argumentative, he is petty and you can tell that he tries not to smile. He walks as though he owns the ground. Ordinarily, this would not be a problem because, in truth, anyone can be loud or crude or narcissistic in some way, to some degree, at any particular time though some people more than others. In this case, however, his presence is a problem. Those who walk in my direction are forced to change direction to avoid walking into him. He stands upon the sidewalk as if it were a conquered nation and his presence is enough to force those who pass—those I see from the vantage point of my window and claim as my own—to avoid me, leave me, disengage from me. The landlady's son forestalls the only opportunity I have to behold and consider the miracle of some other person, some stranger, some being who has a personhood all his or her own. He repels all those who would otherwise enter my life and command my attention and serve as points of wonderment albeit from a distance. He destroys those possibilities. He trespasses upon my psychic space as well: though the evening doesn't belong to him, the thought of him is enough to disrupt the delicate stillness and quiet harbor of my own inner peace. He upsets the panorama of light and air and stars in the night that comprise my universe and he upends the reverie in which I may be immersed. If he were to stand below my window and laugh or scream or berate his mother, his life would thereby be imposed upon my own—and so it is: he disrupts both her life and my life in this fashion. He imposes himself upon my personal eternity, he upsets the array of opportunities that are open to me at any given moment and, as he does, he squeezes my life into smaller and smaller compartments. Because of him, I cannot contemplate or confound myself with the mystery of trains or motorcycles or planes that I might otherwise hear in the distance. I am prevented from contemplating or understanding those who happen to be walking along the sidewalk or rolling down the tracks or passing through the clouds or speeding down the highway as the sound of wheels and engines split the night. My mind is pulled like a moon caught in gravity's grasp so that it circles about him and is bombarded by his statements and exhortations. The space we share is sliced to shreds by his shrill, razor-edged voice. Simply stated, I am dislodged from my world through his presence and I'm hurled into his. My incessant effort to come to terms with my own world is upended.

There is another matter of concern and that matter is a dream that recently visited itself upon me. I had a dream, most of which I can remember, and it was truly a memorable dream. I dreamed that I was lying in bed and, as I lay there, I lifted my head above the windowsill and I looked down upon the street and noticed someone who slowly tilted her head, up, up, up until she was looking straight up at me and our eyes connected. It was a person I didn't know but her smile resembled that of the landlady's daughter. I studied her face and realized that the face before me was a face that I've been waiting many years to behold and I stood up and leaned out and gleefully yelled, "How are you?" in as loud a voice as I could muster. I was joyful and I didn't care the hour and didn't care if I disturbed the entire neighborhood with the sound of my voice. I dreamed that she saw me and received my greeting and yelled in as loud a voice as she could muster: "How are you?" and it went on from there. It was as happy an occasion as I can recall and it was a beautiful thing and I cried in my sleep and I felt the drip of a tear as it ran across my cheek and jumped over my nose into my pillow. At that moment, I woke up and remembered my dream in minute detail and this was quite unusual because I rarely remember my dreams. I retained her image in my head and even though she was a creation of my own mind as it swam in sleep, I nevertheless thought of her as real. I thought about her often and I can't help but think of her often. Though her visit was not real, I spend time wishing she'd reappear. I want her to search for me and find me. I need to hear her cry out, "How are you?" as if it were a statement and, if I were to hear those words, I would respond, "How are you?" and I would luxuriate in her words and she in mine.

In addition to the matter of the landlady's son and the matter of my recent dream, there is the more pressing matter of the landlady herself and the rent which lies at the core of our relationship. In the absence of my obligation to pay rent, there would be no landlady and there would be no landlady's son. She exists, of course, and has a place in my life and has had a place in my life for longer than I can dream or remember. If she did not exist, I would have some other reality to cope with. I might live somewhere else, in some other town or city or in some other room or attic or cellar. I might not spend most of my day peering out a window and, in that event, my eyes might not have the opportunity to lock onto the back of some unsuspecting stranger and I might not lie in the bed in which I presently lie while lost in the sound and mystery of the noise of trains and planes and motorcycles as the sound cascades into the plasma of the night. I might live somewhere else and, for all I know,

I might be someone else. I might be well connected, socially adept, well-liked, sought after, loved. I might owe rent to someone else and might have to answer to someone else but in a different way than at present or I might own my own home in which case I would answer to no one. The possibilities are limitless but my reality, my only reality, is one in which I am bound to a person who has been my landlady for as far back in time as I can remember, to the extent I am able to remember. Her need for me to pay rent emanates from her core and that need is palpable and endless. In order to extract a check from me, she seeks me out and listens to me and cajoles me and soothes me and encourages me and insults me and this has been the case for countless years. She can be kind, she can be understanding, she can be demanding, she can be disagreeable but she doesn't know me and doesn't seem to want to know me but I suspect, in her case, that there is more to the story than her overriding need for me to pay rent. She has tired eyes. She draws her brown-red hair in a bun one day but lets it fall upon her shoulders the next because, perhaps, she lacks the strength to twist it. There are times at which she seems lost as when her voice is weak and her eyes are red and the glistening edge of a tear appears beneath one eye, then the other. I can determine for myself that she feels defeated as when her left shoulder sinks lower than the right and her cheeks appear pale and the laces collapse upon the tops of her shoes with every step she takes, over and again, as if those laces share the burden of her defeat. I think I can tell when she is sad though I say nothing and firmly believe that I shouldn't say anything. I'm tempted, during the course of her visits to ask, "How are you?" but I hold back. It feels wrong or ill-timed or inappropriate or all of these at once. I wish not to take the chance because, if I were to ask, "How are you?" she may not answer and that would be devastating. I won't try, I just can't, I know how it may go and it terrifies me. The question that I could ask is a question that can't be asked. I have a strong sense that she has a multiplicity of needs that shroud themselves within a panoply of selves that cohabit within her but all this is based upon conjecture and the bits of things I've observed that I think I remember. It is all part of my experience and it feels like dejection.

There is, however, the approach that I devised in my own mind based, to some degree, upon memory and dream and an element of hope which is a small raft in a large sea, difficult to cling to but the only thing one can hold onto if one wishes to avoid drowning. That hope will become a reality because I see it in my mind's eye. I am certain of it and I can say with utmost assurance that the event or experience I contemplate will happen as though it has already happened. It cannot refrain from happening: it wants to happen and, therefore, it is bound to happen. Reality bends in my direction, it has no choice, it can be no other way just as history has no other option but to be whatever it is, at least to the extent that it can be retrieved or remembered or dreamed. What will happen is this: I will peer out my window and see a blue dot at the end of the street and that featureless blue dot will grow and advance in my direction. That blue dot will define itself and come closer and take on the features of a human being and, before long, I will not see a blue blur but will see, rather, the landlady's daughter once again. She will approach in her wheelchair from far, far down the street and I will recognize her and find comfort in her familiar image. I will remember her, to the extent that I am able, in the form and manner of the person she is and I will recognize the array of bits and pieces of her that have lingered in my memory. The woman I see will be the same person as the girl I once knew. I will realize that she's been gone, long absent, deeply missed and I will suddenly realize how much I've missed her. I will realize her as a person, here and now, in the course of this new time, this new immersion, this new day. She will come from the far end of the street to my front door, closer and closer, and I will feel the dull vibration and hear the screech and moan of the silver wheels of her steel wheelchair as those wheels cry, louder and louder until, finally, that screech and moan ceases. She will sit upright in that chair and I will see her situated directly below the sill of my window and she will allow the wind to lift grey tufts of her hair so they float like feathers above her head as the air lurches past her in spasms and her hair will rise just high enough to reveal bright earrings, each laden with glassine diamonds that light electric, energized by the spears of the sun's light that land like arrows and those glistening targets will fire like bolts of twisted lightning against the coral sky. I will slowly lift my head above the windowsill and slowly stand and I will feel the gentle push of the airstream against my face and beneath my hair and around my shoulders and my features will be clear and evident for her to see and she will ask "How are you?" and I will respond, "How are you?" and I will let those words fly in the air in a manner in which they can be heard and felt and understood and they will be heard and felt and understood as a statement and they will mean and can only mean, "I need you."

City People, Country People

City people are radiant,
Country people ashen;
City people live like kings,
Country folk go hungry.

City people wear fine clothes,
Jewels like tiny suns;
Country people wear threadbare rags,
Crowns of twig and weed.

City people never dream,
No rapture in their sleep
But country people
Dream of silver seas
And mountains made of gold.

Headstones

Pity those headstones by the road:
They languish in the crowded yard;
They guard their dead, stand vigil over them
Like sentries massed in perfect rows,
But never do they speak among themselves
Out of fealty to those who lie beneath.

Abandoned, left alone to persevere:
No family left to care for them,
No sons or daughters in the lineage
To lay flowers at their feet
On a Sunday afternoon
Or clear away the weeds;
They are orphans now.

The old grey slab stands alone,
Hidden in the corner:
It leans like some old uncle,
Knees and ankles misaligned,
Features cracked and rearranged,
Waist worn thin, shoulders bent,
Its skin grown rough and pale,
The name no longer legible;
Chiseled words and numbers
Recede like memory,
Lost in the pyre of age,
And forgotten are the dates
That once were clearly etched
Upon the front like a person's face
That grew tired and absurd
In the months before he died,
A face that mocked the face
That he once wore
When he was young
And ruled the world,

Long before he understood
That he, in time, would die.

There will come a day
When the very last man
Will leap across a gravel patch
Where once a headstone stood,
Planted so long ago
By a broken, arrogant few
To demark the life of one they loved
For the rest of time to come
But whose name will be lost before too long;
And when that runner has run his race,
No one will be left to know of humankind itself,
No one to know that men and women
Walked the ground and lived their lives;
New seas will rise and drown the earth
And will flood the yard,
And all those orphan stones
And all those bones and the ground itself
Will wash away, and fish will swim
Where rows of headstones stood;
But, even so, one can't deny that, yesterday,
There lived a man who was alive
And when he lived, his life was real:
A headstone testifies that he existed,
Proclaims the truth of the dream
That was his life, and defines
His soul in space and time
And, for today, at least,
Holds vigil over him.

Tell Me

What will you do when you're too weak to row?
I'll lie upon the open deck and drift along the rippled sea.

How will you cross the sunless beach?
I'll follow the sound of the song of the moon.

Will you crawl through the grassy ground?
Beyond the edge of the mossy field.

Will you sink into the desert sand?
I'll run like mad by the beige baked dunes.

Where will you go when the air gets cold?
I'll sleep beneath the hawthorn leaves.

Will you be lost in the winding gorge?
I will roll with the wind and shall be delivered.

How will you find the ocean's edge?
I'll lie upon the open deck and drift along the rippled sea.

The Secret of the Moon

When everyone has gone to bed
And all are fast asleep,
The moon climbs down from astral space
And sits among the butter cups.

Once he's rested, he wastes no time
But walks along the shore,
Mingles with the chatter fish
To rid himself of loneliness.

When first the sun begins to stir
And morning's grey light flickers,
The moon jumps back behind the clouds,
Careful not to make a sound.

Shadows

In the afternoon, when sun is king,
I walked along the shore;
Three shadows followed me,
Each one longer than the next.

The first was child in adult form,
Groping for a hand to hold;
Sinking steps in yellow sand;
The sweater he wore had once been mine;
I buttoned it up so he wouldn't catch cold
And did my best to arrange his tie;
It made me cry as we walked along.

The second was worldly,
Propelled by the tide
Of habit and experience,
Pale with fear despite the sun,
Furrows deep along the brow,
Creases in the cheek,
Desire dried and cauterized
Long before he had reached the beach;
It made me cry as we walked along.

The third was a shepherd,
Sober eyes, solemn pout,
Crooked neck and head bent forth;
He'd lean upon his walking stick,
Bronze wood scarred by wind and salt;
He lifted it up when the sun turned red
And pointed to the mountain ahead,
Dim blue edifice, azure crest
And, all at once, we all looked up;
It made me cry as we walked along.

Steamship

I couldn't find the pier. It was hidden somewhere along the trembling edge of my cold town. It was out of sight, beyond my reach and all the while the boat was waiting. I lost my way among dizzy streets, crisscross straight or winding out but no wharf in sight whichever way I turned. Time had run and it was now certain that I would miss the boat. I would be left behind while the great ship propelled resolute toward deep water, farther away with each passing moment.

No steamship to take me where I needed to go. I thought I saw it retreat from the infirm pier but that vision was one that rose and fell only in my mind's eye. In fact, I was nowhere near that boat when it left but I could feel it pull away from the land the very moment the lines were hauled in and coiled like gold ringlets upon the deck and the whole of it slowly drew away in search of open sea. And though I had never seen that boat, I knew that it was meant for me. I was born to be in it, on it, part of it, so it seems to me.

It was a steamship of the old sort, one of the great boats of a dying breed: sleek and fast, tall stacks and high decks, name blazoned in large white letters across either side of the bow. It had been built by men who were desperate for something to revere, some means to leave the land, some way to be a part of the sea or part of the night that they would scour with huge searchlights that would cross the sky with long wands of light that wavered back and forth like the arms of some incandescent metronome. This was their way of searching, yearning, needing, seeking, engaging in holy mission.

The deep throated horn would bellow loud and all would hear that clarion call as ships left port and slid easy atop the green slate sea and blue smoke overflowed those mammoth stacks and climbed the lattice sky, slowly turning grey, then white, then lingering in air, hanging from the heights like dangling threads, trailing behind, dissipating, fading out until they were gone. Those boats churned the water, steel-sided, heavy buoyant, old alive, riding high like a coach-and-four through a concourse they carved upon the seething surface. They routed the water along straight lines and were so large that they could hardly have been imagined back in those ancient days when the sea always had the final word. Their hulls were perfect and imposing and they slipped easily through storm after storm, defying winds and waves, rushing fast forward like some winged holy venture. They ran at speeds we can't imagine today and they wouldn't slow or stop until they had reached the faraway shore. There was nothing to hold them back and they roved the ocean unimpeded.

Their grandeur was deeply ingrained in thick grey steel. They wore their colors like simple suits, red and black, and each side etched with a perfect white waterline that cut straight across as if seared by some holy brand. Their masts would rise up out of the sea, high above the deck and would glisten like long, righteous swords that reflected angular shafts of light that would cut through the salt air like the beams God sends crashing through stained glass on Sunday: that same hard, true light that sifts through men's dreams so that those who sleep can see the life they are denied in the course of a day.

Such a boat had been berthed in wait for me and such a boat would have carried me along but it left the wharf without me. Now it runs from me with increasing speed and is many miles, countless miles, from the small scrap of ground upon which I stand, purposeless, my temporal skin and transitory thoughts stacked like loops of rope in a pile upon the dusty posts of my weak legs.

I was left behind and lost. I was just another casualty and I simply retreated. As I did, I had a vision. I saw life in all its forms: life winding through houses, huts, tents and buildings, wide forests and long deserts, all of it at once, all life that lived within and on the earth, all that breathed, all mortal things. I saw the great multitude, I saw the grand array, a huge bevy spinning all so fast, like trembling life, life on the fly, a swirling carousel. The highest buildings spun, faster, faster, wouldn't stop and the fields spun and so did the lakes and mountains and the frozen snow. The whole world spun upside down, in every direction, and picked up speed and I knew my world, once so still and somnambulic, would never be the same. It would now be one that could only spin, too fast, too hard, too harsh, too cruel, up and down and lost in the mass of a jumble and all of it would be thrown and fall and fly about like leaves in the windy corner. All those earthly things that I once knew turned sharp and cold, all in a splutter and everything and all spun like rotors in motion, too fast to be understood by a single set of eyes. Buildings spinning like dancing bricks: it makes no sense unless you see it. Spinning fast like a turnabout clock, a broken basket of life in a box, twisted inhuman, as fast as the wings of a hummingbird and brittle like marbles in a bag thrown high and dropped, falling hard and all those people chipped and cracked like broken marbles, each against the other, damaged and disconsolate.

And so the flowers spun and the yellow petals of sober daisies circled round like eyelet stars, paper sharp propellers on the wing and, oh, those trees were cruel and their branches jutted out, cutting edges, inhuman consequence like a rip saw at work, dangerously close like a meteoric storm: those blades were sharp and angry and voracious. The birds spun too, above my head as well. They flew in flocks that wandered and weaved in circles in air, denied a place to land. The world was a spinning storm, lost in a throbbing cyclone, dancing against its will in every conceivable direction.

I was the one who couldn't spin. I just wobbled scared, like the last stalk of wheat in a barren field, completely lost this time: no water, wharf, road or tunnel but knowing now that an ancient edifice had come and gone and never would it come again.

I thought I saw the last traces of smoke rising toward the floor of heaven but, no matter what I saw, a vessel bolts like a fugitive through the thrashing sea at ungodly speed and will soon be too far away to remember. It breaks across unchartered water like a plow through virgin ground while I am left behind. I bide my time upon the broken bric-a-brac in a world that spins around me. I have no rail upon which to lean, no life preserver onto which to cling but all the while I am falling over, tripping into ceilings that once were floors. I am abandoned for all the time that I have left, knowing now that I will never see the rippled water and steamy waves and ancient oceans and curved rivers and all those silent lakes that lie beneath the land, estuaries warm and infinite, waters known or waiting to be found.

Whatever Might Be There

"Yesterday, I walked along the empty corridor that lies behind my consciousness and opened up a door—

And what I saw astounded me

> *An endless room of empty space, open and alive, black velour in layers, one atop another, each one darker than the next, lit by all these tiny stars, blinking white and ultra-bright, embellished borders rife with planets (at least a dozen, more or less), dressed in golden overcoats, sometimes red or raw sienna, tilting spinning leaning tops; they wandered through that space as if it were a park*

And then, today, I walked along the shore, determined legs, swinging arms and felt the tension in my hand and simply decided, then and there, to open up my fist—

And what I saw astounded me

> *A butterfly flew out, magenta rose and tiny pink chapeau atop, perfect legs and wings pressed thin like cotton cloth, single yellow stripe from end to end and each veined blue and powdered white like coffee cake, amber dotted all around, flutter fly and off she went*

Which is why I suggest that you might not know what lies in wait— and I tell you, stranger, I did not—but isn't it just possible that a room waits, patiently, for you to step inside?

Do your fingers long to reveal the gifts you've held in hand for far too long?

Is it fear or gravity of thought or weight of flesh that suffocates the life in you?"

The City

Cold ground,
Bleach dry sky:
I left my home
In search of the city.

I walked for days
Past hazy hills,
Pastel fields
And masted boats
Asleep in the harbor.

I walked
A perfect line,
More or less,
And when I came
To the very end,
The city loomed
In front of me.

Harsh noise fell hard
Upon my head;
Great grey monoliths
Leaned against the sky;
They lurched like
Shrugging shoulders
As men and women
Scurried through the street;
Life interspersed
Among the ruins:
Dim faces,
Languid eyes,
Heaving humanity,
Dire choices,
Dearth of meaning,

Loneliness and cruelty
Through the long course of day
And cold, interminable night.

I have walked
A thousand miles;
I have shed my past,
I have no home,
I am caught in the grip
Of the city's gravity;
I feel its drag;
I'm drawn along
And I am done,
I have journeyed
All this way
To find myself
Lost among the ruins.

Deep into the Night

Years ago, when I was small,
My father, every other night or so,
Thinking everyone asleep,
Would sneak out of the house
And climb into his motorboat,
A leaky wreck that wreaked of oil;
He'd rip the cord and run full bore,
Drive it deep into the night.

He'd push that boat beyond its limit,
Running rampant on the sea,
Looking for a storm,
Longing for the chaos in it:
Tornados on the waves,
Thrashing water twisters.

He'd head straight toward the breakers,
Lightning popping all around,
Inspired by the thunder,
Blinded by the rain,
Spat upon by angry waves,
Shoved aside by the vulgar swells;
He'd ride as far as he could go,
Hardly able to steer that boat,
Just about to fall apart
But he simply didn't care:
Bottle in hand, he'd tip it back,
Drink it in, shriek and moan
Like a man gone mad,
Feeling what he needed to feel,
Barely coming home alive.

◊

Years ago, when I was small,
My mother, every other night or so,
Thinking everyone asleep,
Would fill herself with gin
And sneak out of the house,
Walk up to the highway,
Slip between the speeding cars
And walk the double yellow,
Heel to toe, unsteady along the center line.

A thousand drivers, unsuspecting,
Sped toward her on either side;
They'd pass within a breath of her,
Bottle in her left hand,
Leopard handbag in her right;
Drivers doing 80
Veered over if they saw her
And miss her by an inch;
Honking horns and epithets:
If she heard, she couldn't care less,
Feeling what she needed to feel,
High wire act on solid ground,
Suborning death with ambivalence,
Always lucky to get arrested;
Sometimes the cops would bring her home.

◊

They are long gone, those two;
They have left me to myself
And I miss them terribly,
As terrible as that may sound
Which is why, at times,
When I can't sleep,

(Every other night or so),
I turn on the light
And sit at my desk,
Place sheets of paper
In front of me,
Lift my pen and write,
Compelled by rabid need
And longing without end:
Countless poems, countless lines,
Countless pages in a pile,
Countless hours as the hours add up,
Deep into the night.

Time in Mind

I have in mind a kind of time
That can't be measured by clock
Or monitored by calendar;

Time that isn't tucked away
In packages of seconds, days or centuries;

Doesn't start when you wake up
Or wait for you while you're asleep;

A different species altogether,
Hard to figure out:

Time like moonscape chaparral;

Time as dark as unlit streets;

Time as bright as an angry sun
That stares at you at noon
But loses sight of you at night;

Time as quiet as a curtain rod
That clutches the curtain from year to year
But lets it swing in the languid breeze;

Time like eyelet stars,
Woven through the fabric of night;

Bodies of time through which we swim
From the shallow end of morning
To the landing of the night;

Time that lies in wait for you,
Hidden in the desert,
Deep among the creases
Of the sunbaked sand.

I have in mind a kind of time
That can't be understood
But pulses through the ether:
Tip tap footsteps through the hall;
Boats bouncing on the rumpled sea;
Yawning morning, coral pink,
Streaks of grey in the afternoon;
Winding road of cobblestone.

I Saw a Mountain

A mountain stood upon the spot
Where I now stand;
Relieved of cliffs it once embraced,
Beaten to death,
Crushed beneath the wheel,
Its permanence denied;
It is gone, it is lost within an ocean
That neither you nor I can see;
Nothing left but an image
Etched upon the plate of memory
Which fades a little more
Each time it is recalled.

Its atoms tremble in the night,
Thrown for miles by random winds
And dropped upon the desert floor:
They are ashes, they are dust,
They are the mountain I once saw.

◊

I saw a mountain in my mind,
An imposing monument
And, in a moment, I saw it die.

That vision would not submit
To the words and thoughts
That marched through my mind
In close formation;
Reason drowned in a sea of what I saw;
I couldn't move and, in my panic,
Sought comfort in the myth
Of lineal experience;

I looked for reassurance in my belief
That something follows something else
And every moment supersedes
The river of moments that came before,
But I found no solace in that conceit:
It made no sense to me.

◊

I am lost upon the very spot
Where a mountain died so long ago,
Whose heavy bones were ground to sand
And yet I see it still: I see a mountain
Where none exists and I see, as well,
The shifting dunes that stand in place of it;
A mountain crumbles, grain by grain,
But, even so, I also see
A thousand moments thrown together;
A mound of sand becomes a stair;
I take a step and then another;
I climb, I rise, I walk from star to star
And, far below, I see a world I never saw:
A sprawling forest grows
Where once a mountain stood.

A Lion in the Village

I alone standing, full of mood, heavy with need and I was longing all along, all upon the great savannah where the village sits. Grassland wide and flat from here to there: it was once whatever it was and then became whatever it became, different than before, of a kind that should be green but yellows with thirst in time and stiffens like brush, each thin blade sharp spikey and the grand array of parched trees distant, sagging robes of countless leaves, very dry, each and every, hanging from the branches, yellow edged and thin lined brown along the crisscross veins.

Old man talking some, yelling some, all alone like me alone but I and he right there among the all of us and I consumed with crushing concern and this concern, so much of it, has flooded over me and I drown in it, sick of it, stuck in it, caring so much and that's what happens. Coarse grass, petulant heat, eats you up and I am trapped, trapped in the coarse grass and heat and the harsh light and pain of caring, my ears and eyes and all my ailing senses tired, failing senses, failing flanges, sound and sight and thought and feel and all that longing falling to the ground and there it seeps belabored. And people, I and him and they, all and all, we sit in a circle upon our sitting mats, old mats woven in the long course of time by ancient aunts and uncles, carefully sewn intricate, delicate thread, sun and moon, mountain and sea, blue and green, yellow and red, long ago when there was time to weave and they, the ancient aunts and uncles, now long gone, had time to rest and weave and rest again while sitting or lying by the bubbling brook in the warm and cool spring breezes while grass grew soft and new, all around, and reached them like the light reply of a lazy ripple of a lazy sea that meets your foot at the very, very edge, reverses course and heads back out and rejoins the sea, countless ripples drifting out rejoining, each like the gentle breeze you longed for and leaves you standing, waiting for the next but now, this now, right now, the grass perfectly dry in a painful way and no doubt destined to wilt in time and cease being grass and you could see the not-so-green now-flayed-yellow twinge like rusted fire ember and I could see it and feel it as I touched the dry ground while sitting on my sitting mat. I was waiting, so much so, hungry sleepy scared but more mood than hunger and more hunger than scare though it seemed to change often like flavors of a soup convoluted with the stirring of the ladle, convulsed as one but not quite one and now the even flow of rich memory and sense of moment embraces you from the inside like wine that lulls you into snore-sleep, leaves you alone, leaves you not needing but, in fact, you need even more, all the while disconsolate and you hardly notice, overwrought you are, undermined by an undercurrent, a quirking lurking underneath, the long unsettled moment. The man over there was an elder, one of the fine and wise but no finer or wiser than us because he was as unhappy like us, seemingly lost, no more no less than me and the others though obvious in his case as age had crushed the he who he once was, bereft of sense of where or what, no real question, no complaint but, all the same, unhappy and you could almost see a dismal ether rise like steam from out his mouth in words incoherent and the sudden jerk of shoulder and lurch of arm, left to right and back again, clenched fist but no real answer and eyes peering, left to right like gates that swing and then they blink and blink again, open and close, lids up and down like old thatch doors where long ago the grain was stored. Now was a different time, it is true, true for me in this now, the now that everyone knows though a bit different for each and every he and she, you and me, it cannot be the same, each living and breathing at different distance, different angle in the course of the long moment of experience, each his own, a different each in every case or so I surmise but cannot know, different points in the long unwinding, each different from the next, one grain of the many grains, one drop of a heavy rain, a flicker in the beam of light that gleams forever but bends around the high heavy things, the hills and plateaus but then falls off, long after you've come and gone, traveled back and forth and back again during loss and hope, the cry and laugh through the long drone of in-between, a conversation that gropes along and ends in time, decides little, yields nothing in the long course. You are connected and then alone, wholeheartedly alone, in the grip of where is mother, all in the blink of an eye and you are diverted, desperate for something, that special something, something you need and search for in ways you know and ways you hardly realize, something other, something else: you yearn for it, a something that your eyes cannot harbor and your ears cannot hear and your mind cannot design and can't find in the cavern of self, mine or yours or anyone else's though it always ought to be there. I drink the water, the little left in my old stone cup and the ten or twenty or thirty of us all sit in the same way or so we did, heavy upon our mats, lifting stone cups from time to time and drinking in random order, too hungry to move, too long in one place in one time at one time, expanding now to include the then and that which was to come and, certainly, I was beset by too much mood. It comes over me from time to time in the same way it seems to overtake others, now and then, but it's still my own, your own, can't be discarded or consigned or shared with another someone sitting on a sitting mat near your own that looks like yours. Lonely I was. I was lonely in the heart of that throng, those who knew me, those who loved me and all those I loved and, then and there, I felt the primordial trembling moment, the long ago first thinking feeling self and I saw the then and now of so long ago and beheld a vague sense that I was walking through grass, a memory like mist but I do recall that the grass was blue-green like a river but now the moment, all jumbled up, was more like a tremble that comes upon you quietly and leaves slowly, a moment that used to be a single point in a long line of points often interrupted, often tangled, not perfectly straight and all this as the shepherdess walked by, right by, she with the dark scar upon her cheek like a pierced deer, she with the rose lips pressed grim tight. She pretended that her sheep and cows and goats still follow, one after another in long line that long ago stretched far, far back and all those sheep and cows and goats would follow her like a mother and there were calves and lambs that followed as well, generations of offspring in so long a line as to seem endless. They would join her without summons and never stray but we could see as she marched along that she was alone and had no followers and her children were gone and none were left: there were no sheep or cows or goats and we saw this and pitied her, watched her walk alone, leading a parade that wasn't there. We saw her stare, straight and resolute, as if eyeing some place or other, far away in order to reach it, drawn, perhaps, by some distant living thing that she imagined she saw, a destination far away but in front of her which she preferred to pursue rather than slow the course, turn her head to the left or right, lean back and dare notice the extent of her loss, realize that her children were gone, fathom the fact that she was now alone, absorb the trauma of her tragedy, scream or cry or fail to cry but stagger back and collapse beneath the delicate blue hue of a wrinkled sky like a grimace beneath a twisted brow.

Out of my eye, I saw the top of the crisp grass, now brown faded, dull with thirst, endless field and on and on, dry like empty sea, water long gone. There were acacia trees and jackalberry far away and you could see some of those branches, long and heavy, somewhat curved but angular, random jagged against the blue gaunt like arms thrown wide in wild array when there is no answer and nothing left to do but throw up your hands and continue to wait, the moment then and the one now merging in one long now: you can hear them collide, the one and other, a dull thud like jackfruit falling from branches hard upon the ground and I realized it doesn't really matter where you are or where you sit or why or when it is. The place is always a place, some place, that same place as if it were one place that you carry around, one or another and it is always a time, some time, the same time you carry around and when I walk, I walk now and now I walk and I am here and now I am there, somewhere,

89

I am, I am here and there, one place or another, one time or another, all the same, not that far from anywhere nor much later than before.

And sitting there, not quite still and not quite not, I longed for something while sitting on a sitting mat woven by my ancient aunt and uncle in the moment that preceded the moment that I became alive and those that followed, all those moments having conspired together to form one long moment, a single array that had no stop or start but ran round unending like a silver ring, perhaps over time but a ring nonetheless. I longed for shade, relief from the heat, something divine to intervene in order to shield me from the insensible sun and I imagined shade like thin shafts of cool night that might protect me from all that is wrong, not so much in the world but in me, all that is wrong within the deep of me, all those things that are really one thing, one overriding matter, the burden I carry which is, namely, my insatiable need, my limitless need, the need that extends beyond my body and mind, intimate need that goes beyond my need for food and water. My need was a need for something else, something sublime, at least as far as I could tell. I needed food and water, of course, but I felt nagging need for that something higher and better, something that could fill me up in a way food and water could not. I wanted to feel my inner emptiness dissipate. This was my basic premise, my raison d'être, and I sought a way to feel the world open up but it hadn't yet happened for me and I didn't know if it could happen, at least for me, at least for now. I felt empty all the time and I call it empty-all-the-time. I was an empty stone cup; I was a dry cup. And sitting there, not quite still and not quite not, longing for fulfillment, I envisioned a tree on a mountain and I envisioned myself sitting peacefully beneath that tree and, in my mind, I saw leaves and branches hanging heavy all around and those leaves and branches blocked the acerbic rays of a despotic sun and thereby protected my limp lump self and, as I envisioned myself shielded beneath a tree, protected in this way, I looked out into the far away and a dot appeared far out, far away, hardly visible upon the horizon's edge, long distant beneath the acacias overhanging and soon that dot became large and larger as it moved toward me as I, heavy with need and filled with longing, waited for it, longed for it and then and there, in front of my eyes, the lion took shape, walked toward me in languid step, loped slow, unperturbed and unconcerned, so it seemed.

He came right up to me, walked by me, stopped and lowered to the ground until supine upon it and perfectly in place, his rightful place at the very center of the circle of mats upon which we sat. We stared at him for a moment because he was absolutely new, drew our curiosity, but there he was as if he had been there forever like us, not new at all. Now he was here; here he was. I felt secure and all my concern and all my anguish evaporated, faded like fatigue that merges into sleep that comes upon you, converges with the moment, an old moment, this moment made much longer by his presence, much richer, not a new moment but a moment very much part of the long unending moment and I felt safe in the course of the moment that was now. I gleaned the mother in him and I leaned against his sandy skin, curled fur like tangled ermine weed. He stared straight ahead and didn't seem to notice me and, strange to say, I cared no longer, not like before, less beleaguered at that moment. A lion had come to us and together we were, just as though we had come to him. He sat there, next to me and I leaned against him and I relied upon him as would a child. He was the rock upon which I rested and I felt the warm heave of his brown torso and my eyes moist in the rise of the heated vapor that was his breath. His mane tilted to one side like flower bouquet, too heavy and leaning over in the vase but the long strands of it not simply umber or sienna but more than a single color, one or another, a fine array of color carefully arranged like that same bouquet: red and orange, black and white, beige and yellow and shades thereof and many others, each very different or just a bit different, one from the other in the same way that grains of sand are each of a different sort, different shade, different tone and cast, dull or gleaming, one way or another, subtle strains of color, sometimes this or that but never the same. That mane with all its fine shades was very much a color weave, strands of sandy string, kaleidoscopic everchanging when and where you looked, exploding desert coloration. I looked down at his paws which were wide and heavy like roots of trees that spiral into the ground and disappear and never move but you know are there. When he turned toward me (and he did turn toward me), I could see his nose, flesh red triangle upside down and eyes that were green-black ingot round. I was lost in those eyes and loved to peer into them because I could almost see myself and I patted his head. Content I was though he didn't seem to notice but I know he was aware of me and sensed us all and was, perhaps, content himself, as if he knew us long before and all of us were right there with him and wanted nothing more than to lie there, wide circle all around, as close to him as we could be for all the time that we had left and we did not move for the longest time. I leaned freely against his muscled shoulder, broad back, heavy like ancient edifice, massive cats made of stone, faces human and serene like those that wait in the desert for all time to come like forgotten alters waiting to be found. I had no worry in the world and no one else in the world I knew had any worry of any sort, as far as I could tell.

It was soon, very soon, after he took his place among us that a brook bubbled up, rose out of the ground. It came from a distance and emerged not at once but progressively as it channeled through the ground like a rolling ball but avoided us, curved around us, continued to run long into the horizon toward the spot from which the lion had first emerged. Passive it was and it gushed forth gently, hardly surprising to any of us that a brook had risen out of the dry dust ground after waiting so long to emerge and was now liberated, flowed unabated in the open air and breathed once more like long ago. It bubbled arrhythmic and the sound was soothing to me: I had never heard such beauty. Though it curved around us, it was close enough to cool the air, sojourn by and away, not at all a slow slurry but quick and clear over almond rock and black earth pebble, small white caps from time to time rushing irregular jutting left right toward the horizon and far away trees to revive them, helpless in the distance, roots long tangled in the dead ground, long waiting patiently and we were far away but we could clearly see it all, so precisely, dry brown leaves suddenly green and purged of all that was old and despairing and yellow and dull. Gone were the black dapple dots that blighted and, in that moment, we saw new leaves burst forth, so many, twisting nubile out of the tiny twigs of the branches that held the cusps that blossomed as if those leaves could not help but be born and could not be held back, couldn't help but be spun like silk from buds that cloistered over the length and breadth of branches that now gave birth to them, new long leaves that waved up and down as branch arms danced en masse in the cool breeze while all around us the grass sprouted up, this time blue-green, yellow wilt no longer but soft carpet, lush luxuriant and we sat right there upon our sitting mats in the cool by the water as breeze traversed by each of us through the bevy that was us. The sun dulled its piercing light, now easy upon our eyes, not blinding but kind and we wanted nothing, needed nothing and we listened to the bubbling water as it flowed by us toward the thin line distant that separates sky and ground. We watched the grass rise and the birth of leaves and we listened, said little and a vision briefly arose in my mind of lions resting in distant fields.

The lion didn't eat, the lion didn't sleep and we didn't eat and we didn't sleep but we sat in a circle for the longest time, lion at the center, our ancient mats like new rewoven. The shepherdess came upon us, she with the dark scar upon her cheek like a pierced deer, she with the rose lips grim tight, parading through, emerging out of nowhere or so it seemed, a long line of sheep and cows and goats trailing behind her, single file, calves and lambs as well, all ages and sorts, vigorous, healthy, bleating aloud and following her like mother reborn right along the edge of the brook toward the distant

93

trees. She turned her head looking back over her shoulder to see that none were lost and they were all there, none were lost. They came and went and we watched the come and go, but I turned away from the sight of them and turned toward the lion and he turned to me and I stared into the deep well of his ingot eyes and I looked into that deep pool in the same way I sometimes stare into the night when stars beckon and, in that moment, I saw the hot embers of all my yearning fall into those pure, calm waters and those embers cooled and I was living in the depth of the moment and it felt like ancient lions roaming, like the end and beginning of grace long in coming or a river that runs forever, like the eternal embrace, like the end of moments, the end of need, all as it should be, an end of place and the winding down of the course of time and nothing left to do but lie supine upon the grass like a child in the world, like the first child and like the last as well, like a mother lost no longer, like love never known now known, now realized: love like a deep river. I was sated and turned away and so did the elder who was now assuaged, no longer talking, no longer yelling, not seeming alone. The lion jumped, sprang from his legs straight up and came down four square upon the ground and rolled in the grass plush soft and we raised our arms high in the air, danced in circles and jumped for joy and then we rested and savored the moment, savored the cool air, a salve that consoled us without a word, without a thought and relieved the ache of our necks and faces and we savored the white sky and the blue fade of it and the cinnamon streaks of late day against it, long lines and wide arcs. We savored all of it, he and us, and we were quite happy like children in the world, like first and last child, like all those who wait, like ancient aunts and uncles and all those who are just now born, like ancient souls, like all who are living and all their children and all who love them, all known and never known, love deep like a river rife with flux and tussle, lunge and pummel, propelled by unfathomable currents through the unchangeable moment that doesn't stop and doesn't start and we all rested and were happy, he in the center surrounded by us and we on our sitting mats.

All this came about until a moment came, a long moment that caused me to need again and care again and again I was concerned. I thought I saw the brook itself recede and sink, ever so slightly, and I thought I noticed the flow of water slacken, just a bit, and though I had no idea where the shepherdess had gone, I came to believe that she had lost her way and it wasn't long before I believed that her children were lost as well. I placed my hand upon the lion's neck and I was disturbed because it was no longer thick with fur but was sparse, some there, some not and I patted his shoulders which were spotty with fur in patches and his skin felt cooler than before though he seemed not to notice me and we all took turns standing over him, all of us caring and peering down and we could see the barren patch widening, pocked skin now uneven raw as clumps of fur dropped to the ground and rolled or collected or scattered in the breeze like leaves across the savannah, this way and that, away from him and us. We did not know what to do and, just then, just now, his eyes were grey film covered and they fell beneath parched lids which shut like doors. We could not see his eyes but he breathes, he sleeps, he leans against me and I against him, my arm over his neck and now both arms all around, long embrace to constrain the life from leaving, now pointless to pray because he is the one, the only one, who could answer a prayer that a lion not die. He is the one, if anyone, to deny death's petition and allay our fear, satisfy our yearning and ease our burden. How to heal the healer, I don't know, no one knows. No matter, I can do nothing but try to warm, slow the cooling, comfort him as best I can and savor the whatever warmth that remains for the rest of his life and mine. He has no mother, I have no mother. In a sudden, I begin to sense the onset of need, an ancient yearning, a want profound, a desperation for that single, simple thing that never was, never could nor now can be. I am in need and overwrought and we are bereft, not knowing what to do, all here sitting and wondering in our hearts what will become of us.

Creation

There is a place where God resides,
A holy temple built of marble, mined
By angels from the depths of heaven,
Pale like alabaster, streaked blood red:
The marrow of eternity.

She sleeps upon a bed of stone;
She doesn't wake, cannot be woken
But as She sleeps, She dreams of
Everything there ever was
And all there is to come.

A vision forms within Her dream:
The end of everything,
The universe destroyed,
An imminent apocalypse
And, as She sleeps, She sees
Eternal ties unravel, the force
That holds the world in place
Surrenders, universal laws
Are broken, the tether snaps
And, in a dream, She sees
The cosmos fall apart:
Moons and meteors collide,
Planets crumble in the tumult,
Galaxies collapse and suns
Are set adrift and drown
In unremitting nothingness
As darkness, once again, prevails
And the world is as it was
Before it was created.

Within Her dream,
She wanders through
The corridors of space,

Strewn with fragments
Of a broken world
Where once the planets
Circled stars like Maypole dancers,
Auroras dyed the night
With subtle strains of violet,
Magenta supernovae
Showered space in brilliant torrents
And herds of roving galaxies
Trampled through the universe.

God stumbled in the dark
But, resolute, She staggered
Through the rubble,
Picked up the pieces
And carried back Her burden:
Meteors and burning bone,
Molten metal, air and water,
Deserts and seas, bits of rock,
Particles too small to see,
Mounds of ash and dust,
Mountain tops and shards of light;
She bore that weight upon Her back
And in the darkness, found Her throne
And sat, and spilled the pieces
In Her lap, and slowly
Fit them back together.

In a dream, She felt, once more,
A trembling ecstasy; She lifted
Up the universe, held it
High above Her head
And gazed upon a newborn world,
Built from the wreckage
Of one that broke apart;

Living stars, like children,
Bathed Her eyes with light;
The world was luminescent,
Brighter than the world that,
Somehow, She had lost.

Fences

Long ago, you played in the yard,
Throwing a ball, running hard;
Peering through the chain link fence,
Scanning fields, green and distant,
Yearning for the hour
That fences could be overcome
By simply climbing over them.

This is who you were back then
But who are you right now?
Those fields were steeper than appeared,
The breeze turned to wind, so unforgiving;
The snow is deep, the sun is sinking
And though you are gone, the going is slow:
It takes the whole of your muscle and bone
To turn to see, so far away,
A tiny yard in disarray
And the rusted fence you left behind.

The River

Come brother, come sister,
Down to the river,
Through the rushes,
Along the banks
And bring the others:
Those who cannot see
And those who gasp for breath,
Those with hands that tremble,
Crumble skin,
Veins that bleed,
Writhing bones,
Those who are insane
And all whose souls are ravished;
Tonight, in the depths of your dying,
I will meet you there.

We will watch the water,
Rushing white, driven by desire,
In search of a blessed sea;
Hold my hand and walk with me,
Alive within the crib
Of night's cool chamber;
Stand beneath the spectral light
And listen to the ancient song
Of the rolling moon across the night.

My Old Dog

Old dog now, for sure, he is:
Chases deer, slower than before
But still he runs.

Wears a mask these days,
Grey beard whisk broom mouth;
Silver fiber undergrowth
Rises through the fur;
Incremental transmutation
Of a coat worn year to year;
"Like a faded shirt," I thought:
It caught my eye one afternoon
But I had not been watching.

A pallor rises from his skin
As though it were a color,
Runs across his hide
Over chin and collar;
Pallid paths around the hummocks
Through muscled corridors;
Threads of gray along his back
But these stripes rise from inside out;
They propagate like moss
Through fallow fields
That once were tan and black
While long white shadows cloud
The granite gorges of his eyes.

He's not as fast as once he was,
Graceless in a rumpled suit,
But his spirit lurks somewhere in there;
He may not know who he used to be
But needs to be who he is right now;
He lumbers, stumbles, unaware
Of that which waits for him:

A hill too far, too steep to climb
Toward which he runs headlong;
He'll run until his mouth is dry
And stagger till his legs are done;
But why does God demean a dog
When, today, the twilight sun
Rains gold upon his brow?
Why ridicule the thing he is
Simply because he saw a deer
And felt, once more, the need to run?

My Eyes Are Small

The portals of my eyes are small
But through them I see the Pleiades,
And when the atmosphere is clear
I see them staring back at me.

My ears are also small:
Narrow halls through which I heard,
One dismal afternoon,
The steady drum of Death,
His footsteps loud upon the stairs;
Steady at first, then tentative,
They slowly faded as Death retreated
For no apparent reason.

In the silence of the morning,
Some trifling sound—a chirping bird,
A broken twig, it doesn't matter which—
Is loud enough to rouse
The mountain from his sleep;
He lets roll the snow
And it decimates a town
That took a thousand years to build.

And so it is that the enormity of love,
Too immense to understand,
Is born within the gentle press
Of pallid lips together,
And the touch of tiny fingertips
Across the boundless space
That lies between two sets of eyes.

Waiting for a Train

In my dying hour,
I fell into a dream
And heard a voice that
Spoke to me in music sound
And each respective sound
Resounded through my mind like words:
Cello crescendo lamentation,
Rising French horn crying,
Tympanic heartbeat through my skin,
Stutter breathing saxophone,
Sympathy in dulcet tone,
Too early to leave,
Too late to die;
Bended note like long regret;
Oboe prayer arpeggio.

I understood those
Music words and,
In my dying hour,
I breathed a final breath
And as I breathed
The voice told me
That a train would come
To take me to the fields of death,
A place to rest for the rest of time
And just as I heard those words
I found myself alive again
(or so it seemed),
Standing on a platform,
Waiting for a train.

I stood as straight
As a dangling chain,
Comfortable, resigned;

No thought, no pain,
Open eyed alert and peering,
Staring at the track in front
And all the track in back;
Roving eyes like searchlights
Up and down those rails,
Keen to see what might be coming
(Nothing at the time);
Nothing to do but stand upon
A spot of stone
Beneath my feet
And breathe and wait
And breathe again.

I stood upon that platform
Waiting for a train
And, in time, the voice
In tempered cornet tone
Sang these words to me:

It rides on silver wheels,
The rods are made of gold,
Its headlight casts a blinding light,
It rolls like thunder through the night.

But in all the time I've waited,
A train has never come
And I wonder if it ever will
Or even if it runs:
Those rails were once connected,
Gleaming silver beams
Set end to end, perfectly aligned,
Rising through the air toward heaven,
Conceived by God, perhaps,
In Creation's aftermath;

But now those rails lie in disarray,
Strewn haphazard on the ground,
Tarnished green and grey, like tin:
They sink in the clay
Of a railroad bed
That once was made of stone.

Are you waiting for a train?
Did you just arrive?
I have waited ever since
Those ancient rails were laid
And I am waiting still;
Today I see the chaos
That time has wrought
In increments,
And a train can't run
On broken track
Regardless of its speed or size;
Hope is simply not enough
To drive a train
Through countless miles
Of rutted ground
And the long, inconstant,
Cruel abyss.

This is a sorry epoch,
An age of constant waning
When perfect things collapse
And decompose,
Quite unlike the days of old
When prayer and piety
Fueled furnaces
In which holy rails
Were forged;

The strength that flowed
Through ancient arms
Was long ago consumed
And no one today
Is strong enough
To wield a hammer
High toward heaven,
Bring it down
Upon the gilded spike
And drive it through the ground;
Even a person who had the strength
Would lack the motivation.

Are you waiting for a train?
In this, my dying hour,
I will leave you here:
It is late and I am lost
In this bitter, brittle night;
I think I see the distant point
At which those ancient rails converge
And I will walk in that direction,
Forever if I must,
And if I hear those rolling wheels,
I will sing into the night,
A symphony of song
Comprised of music words,
A song for all humanity;
Staccato notes like labored breath,
I sing as I crawl
Through the valley of death:
Long chromatic moan,
Melodic sorrow all my own.

The Garden of Eden

A search for the Garden of Eden had been considered from time to time but the collective will to find it had never reached a sufficient level to justify the effort. There were some, however, who wished to proceed and there was no shortage of scientists, historians and theologians who entertained the possibility that the Garden, or what remained of it, existed somewhere in the world. On occasion, commissions were established to consider the matter and, periodically, professional associations lobbied for support to search for the site. That interest, however, would wane as quickly as it arose.

Though the collective desire to take on such a project rarely reached significant levels, the notion that the Garden of Eden could, in fact, be recovered did stimulate public imagination at certain times in our history. Whenever interest was generated, the need to find the Garden would sweep over us like a fever and become an obsession. This mania usually occurred during periods of societal malaise or social upheaval and was often relied upon by those in power to deflect attention from the stresses and tragedies of everyday life. The public grows excited when, for example, the sarcophagus of an ancient king is uncovered or the remains of a dinosaur are extracted from the earth. The reality, however, is that it is not until such discovery occurs, usually by accident, that the prospect stirs the collective imagination. Interest is raised when there arises the possibility that the past, memorialized through legend or myth, can somehow be retrieved. The notion that the holy fabric of our identity can be seen and felt is a tantalizing proposition. For some, however, it is a disturbing possibility: evidence of our origin, placed under the lamplight and examined too closely, might cause that fabric to unravel.

From time to time, stories would circulate that the Garden had been found. Now and again, some historian, anthropologist or religious zealot would claim to have wandered into the jungle in search of the Garden and come away with a piece of it. Every few years, much would be made of some purported discovery in the form of a husk of holy bark, for example, or a fossilized apple and so on. Periodically, newspaper headlines would proclaim some fantastic tale of discovery which would quickly be dismissed, typically, as a hoax or mistake. It was quite often the case that the holy remnant—fruit, bark or fern—turned out to be nothing more than rotten vegetation, well preserved but quite ordinary. Often, these findings were the work of profiteers and scientists on the margins.

For bona fide scientists and professionals, a serious search for the Garden was inconceivable. No archeologist, for example, would knowingly squander precious years to plan and carry out such a project. Assuming a person was capable of implementing a search of such magnitude, it is unimaginable that an investment group or government agency would agree to finance such an undertaking, especially given the low likelihood of success. Even if one were willing and able to carry out the mission, how would that person prepare? Where would he or she go to look? How would one even begin?

The momentum of thousands of generations in the course of civilization forces it ever forward. Societies need to progress in order to survive and the collective mind is disinclined to reverse direction and revel in the past. In this case, no one was eager to accept the arduous burden inherent in so questionable a venture as a search for the Garden of Eden. Why take such a huge historical detour simply to satisfy some psychological or philosophical need? It hardly seemed reasonable or appropriate to devote societal resources and energy in a futile effort to reclaim our origin and, in that way, confirm the historical truth of what we already knew. Thus, the excavation of the Garden could not have taken place until there arose a set of conditions that allowed no other option. The project would remain aspirational until the reality of the Garden could no longer be denied.

There came a day, however, upon which the existence of the Garden became irrefutable and, on that day, the mission to retrieve it became unavoidable. The remains of the Garden were located by accident, thousands of years after that fertile ground had been abandoned and left to decompose like a rotting corpse. An old tribesman came upon it while wandering through the desert. He had strayed miles from his home and was lost, perhaps, or may have been on a mission of some sort. He was hungry, thirsty and scared as he walked directionless across sand and scrub. Cold night descended and he was desperate. He collected a few twigs and leaves with which to light a fire. His plan was to dig a small fire pit. On that particular day, in an attempt to survive in a place that wasn't survivable, he crawled upon that freezing sand and dug a few inches in the ground with his bare hands. He dug with all his strength, he dug in a hurry, he dug as if his life depended upon the size and depth of the hole he could create. He didn't realize, in that moment, that he was touching a lost world, one that had disappeared and fallen out of sight, miles and years beyond the scope of collective memory. There was no sign of it, no marker, no monument or outline but, by chance, this one man had brushed up against it. He had located the holy ground that had been buried for an eternity beneath the cruel, barren sand, tortured by the throbbing heat of day and frozen by midnight winds that seemed to emanate out of some arctic netherworld. In an effort to save himself, that tribesman cleared a path through time and liberated the air and soil of our origin.

He reached down and touched the ancient vestiges of the Garden: old seed, bark, bits of branches, leaves and berries, flower and root and other fragments of life's array, all of which were fossilized,

111

sealed and frozen in clay and amber. The detritus of Eden, the remnant of the paradise through which man first walked and breathed, had been waiting for humanity to catch up to it. In the light of day, acres of uneven topography consisting of sorry patches of dirt and dust, hilly with protrusions and pockmarked with gullies, hinted at a world that lay interred beneath windswept sands. The holy trees, vines, ponds, plants, dried streambeds and fossilized animal bones that had slept forever in the depths of the dark ground, beyond the reach of time, now squinted in the light of day. These were remarkable treasures, to be sure, but they also served as harsh reminders of the abundance and beauty of the life that had once thrived and exulted here and had drained into the earth long ago. Man, having been expelled from the Garden, had discarded his primordial self and had staggered into a foreboding future while the Garden, having been abandoned, succumbed to nature's apathy and lay buried in its grave. By chance, man had returned to reclaim it. Word quickly circulated: the Garden of Eden had been located and its existence was, at this juncture, undeniable. The substance of neonate humanity had been waiting for us and had found salvation in discovery. In short, the past was staring at us in the face and we could no longer ignore that reality.

The revelation immediately and completely transformed the way in which we lived. We were, as a people, overcome with elation and the project became our single priority. In a frenzy, an army of scientists, planners, managers and specialists converged upon the desert and, at once, a steady stream of equipment and money surged toward the site through a pipeline that seemed endless. The intensity of activity was such that one could hardly remember a time at which the project had not been operational and ongoing. It is ironic, I note in passing, that the dubious theories of those who had first claimed that the Garden was locatable and reclaimable now constituted the basis upon which respected experts relied. In fact, some of those experts shamelessly credited themselves as having served as

112

longstanding proponents of the mission. I note, in addition, that the vast undertaking that lay ahead of us—retrieval of the garden and its relocation and reconstruction in a manner accessible to the public—was simply assumed but it was questionable, at least in my mind, whether the project was scientifically valuable or beneficial in any cultural or theological sense. In terms of the collective imagination, however, the merit of the mission and the degree of effort devoted to its realization may not be a matter that can be gauged or even understood.

The anthropologists came, accompanied by soldiers, engineers and archivists. The planning itself required the contribution of myriad professionals who conferred on a continuous basis to review findings and determine direction. Early on, a standing order was issued requiring the site to be phased in as slowly as possible, and that order was soon supplemented by an unending series of advisories, directives and regulations. Archeologists constructed walls and barriers with painstaking precision and the shallow field trenches they established were each cordoned off into small plots and subsections. Specialists were brought in to conduct the delicate process of excavation which was carefully orchestrated: field crews would loosen every inch of sand and soil with trowel and spoon, the ground would be exposed to a certain depth and the dig would be delayed until every crumb of the Garden had been gently lifted and packaged. It would take hours and, in some cases, it would require days to extract the tiniest specimen.

Surveyors were urgently needed to establish boundaries, set corners and delineate the features of the Garden and I was one who answered the call. On a day upon which the sun shone cruel and bright, I arrived by helicopter and, as I gazed down from the sky, I was struck by the degree to which that hallowed ground appeared unremarkable. The entire site was nothing more than a craggy patch of rock and sand and it reminded me of leftover crumbs scattered on a plate. I disembarked and realized that I had journeyed to the middle of nowhere. There was no town, there was no city. There was simply the rolling desert upon which a few huts and tents had been planted. Beyond a broad sand plateau, the Garden slept beneath a pale blanket of powder.

It was the most inhospitable location I could have imagined. The heat was unforgiving. Water was scarce, every drop was a valuable commodity and I was perpetually thirsty. I had difficulty walking: my feet would sink into the fine sand and it took focus and strength to lift one foot up and out as the other sank. In time, I learned to take the least number of steps possible to get from one place to another. The air was thin and dry and each breath seemed a minor victory; I celebrated each time I succeeded in inhaling air and forcing it out of my lungs. I learned to avoid looking out toward the horizon because the sun was a ruthless headlight that seemed to have chosen my face as its target. From the first moment of my arrival, I suffered a headache that never left. My daily experience was one which felt as if I had been rolled into a hot blanket. At times, the nights were as cold as the days were hot.

It took some time for me to find my way around the site but, eventually, I grew familiar with my surroundings. I studied the area in the days and weeks that followed my arrival. Though the site seemed dull and unexceptional at first, my impression changed as soon as I came to the pits. I looked down into a wide ditch and I was astounded. Before me lay petrified leaves, vines of incredible length, fossilized flowers, insects trapped in amber and other remnants of a lost world. I stared at those remains and I was mesmerized. It felt as though they belonged to me in some odd way. I was overwhelmed with a sense that I had fallen back, through millennia, toward an old habitat I couldn't quite remember: a home, perhaps, from which I had wandered. I was not so much overcome by a sense of history as I was consumed with a strange sense of fulfillment, an assuagement of a yearning to reconnect with the broad span of life that had receded from conscious memory. I was alive within a dream but one that arose out of some primordial, collective experience or, perhaps, was simply one borne of the mind of the lost child within me: my own sanity demanded some sense of place along the long arc of civilization. I had been consumed by the long, living shadow cast at dawn, a shadow that darkened as I receded into it. That ancient shadow wasn't black or any shade of grey but was, instead, the beige-brown hue of the ubiquitous haze of desert dust.

There were hordes of workers at the site. They wore long cotton tunics and they wrapped their heads with linen scarves that darkened with the silt of the desert as the day wore on. On that first day, I stood in front of my tent and I was astounded by the number of people on the ground. I was overwhelmed, at times, by the constant movement of laborers and equipment. I felt like a citizen of a thriving, active community notwithstanding the isolation of the place and severe conditions that prevailed. I brought out my tripod, level and water ration. I began my work and I exulted in it. I was part of a momentous effort and felt propelled by the great force of humanity that seemed to swim through the sand toward the Garden itself. I dusted off my compass, I aimed my scope, I cleaned my lens and I spent long hours establishing lines with the rest of my crew.

In a sense, my work was no different than the field work that had been typical of my prior professional life but this work was far more demanding. We would wake long before dawn to avoid the heat, wrap our heads with scarves and masks, advance toward the pits and set our instruments. The risk was high: if we charted a path that was but a fraction of a degree off, a whole section of the Garden might be missed and lost forever. I was certainly overcome with a sense of mission: it was not the money so much as the commonality of experience that attracted me. I had a sense that I was returning to something essential within myself. I had enlisted as part of an army

115

driven by a shared desire to circle back to its own ancient conception and I was but one of many who were compelled by an unyielding need to locate, somehow, a moment and place that had been irretrievably lost, long ago, within the deep well of a forgotten epoch. I was a soldier in search of a way to reconnect to a point in space and time that marked the first step in humanity's long march.

Despite the profundity of purpose and consequential nature of the mission, nothing could be accomplished without hard, physical labor. The reality was that the excavation of the Garden required brute human force to proceed. Unfortunately, a reliable source of labor was not readily available in such a barren, remote region. Workers had to be transported to the site, usually by helicopter or in jeeps and trucks that drove through the night in long lines resembling ancient caravans. There was a constant need for excavation crews to be brought in to dig, sift through sand-filled craters, crack through impenetrable rock and, at the same time, carefully tread to avoid stepping upon delicate remains. Crude labor was also needed to haul heavy pallets of dirt and rock to various stations so that trained specialists could inspect the rubble and extract remnants. These workers had no choice but to rely upon primitive tools: there was no access to power here and it was virtually impossible to pipe in fuel or establish electric lines through hundreds of miles of impassable desert. All the work had to be done by hand, somewhat in the manner of those who built the pyramids so long ago. It is worth noting that those ancient builders constructed grand structures in the desert and, in that manner, had marched fearlessly into their own future. We, on the other hand, had returned to the desert to embrace the point from which we had come. Our mission was one of deconstruction and removal rather than one of art and innovation practiced by those bold, ancient architects. Needless to say, the work was grueling and exhausting. We had been reduced, in a sense, to our collective animalic self: we had devoted ourselves to the task of digging through the dirt like moles in pursuit of grubs to survive.

At first, the size of the labor force was sufficient and the glory of participation was its own reward. There was a constant stream of laborers who joined in the effort. However, that supply of incoming labor, initially steady and sizeable, soon dwindled. Those who needed to earn a living became less impressed by the nature of the mission as time went on. The messianic purpose lost its sheen and the work became routinized. Moreover, as more people became aware of the hardship of life in the desert, enthusiasm for the work dissipated. Public interest waned as the project wore on and the project fell behind schedule. Financial support declined, wages suffered as a result and the workforce contracted even further. The labor shortage became so acute as to slow the pace of excavation to an alarming level.

Through deceptive reporting and misleading public relations efforts, the worrisome state of affairs was covered up for a time but, eventually, the word got out. Political leaders and managers agonized over deteriorating conditions. It was essential that the project, now central to our collective character, continue without further delay. It was feared that a halt to the work would lead to political and economic unrest. To forestall a calamity, troops were brought in to assist in the effort. At one point, an entire division was diverted to the site to perform the most rudimentary, menial tasks. Political leaders and project managers understood, however, that the army could not be relied upon indefinitely. The situation grew dire and a tragic reality loomed. After much public debate, outcry and dissension, a fateful determination was made: laborers would be conscripted by force from nearby tribes to save the project.

The brutal decision to employ forced labor was supported by some and decried by others. It was the source of considerable disharmony and profoundly compromised our character as a people. Ultimately, it destroyed the faith we had in ourselves. We had evolved as an enlightened society over the course of thousands of years—or so we thought—and the proposed solution was anathema to so many of us on a fundamental level. It became apparent, however, that this step was the only means and sole hope of relieving a society in turmoil. In an attempt to mollify those who were outraged, it was said that conscription would be "temporary" and would be terminated as soon as the project had been stabilized. Grudgingly, the proposal was accepted by political leaders and public at large. Though various palliative measures were proposed—future reparations, preservation of the extended family unit for on-site workers, limited work hours, liberal leave, etc.—alleviatory measures were omitted from the final conscription order. In any event, the pitiless die was cast: the project would be carried forth through the use of compulsory labor.

The angst and anger arising out of the controversy threatened to undermine stability across all strata of society and it seems ironic, in hindsight, that the solution devised to save the project and restore public confidence served, in fact, to damage societal cohesion and undermine principles by which we lived. Once the decision was made, however, the plan was immediately executed. We sent our military into neighboring tribal villages and a great number of the inhabitants were either lured through deception or forcibly captured and assigned to specialized labor battalions. In some cases, entire families were relocated to the site to support those laborers and family members served as cooks, messengers, launderers and other capacities. Children were impressed into the work force as well and were compelled to carry equipment, serve meals and clean work areas. As more workers were conscripted and a greater number of work crews established, primitive camps were constructed along the perimeter of the site to house and sustain a growing population. In a short span of time, the project became wholly dependent upon compulsory labor. Without the work of a captive labor force, the project would undoubtedly have fallen apart.

It was a truly disturbing development, no doubt the most despicable aspect of the entire venture. Platoons comprised of units of men, harnessed like pack animals, were forced to haul long pallets piled high with rock. I watched this and I was appalled, certainly when I first arrived: I was sickened by the sight of human beings yoked to each other like oxen and forced to tread forward while weighed down by tons of rubble. However, over the course of days, months and years, I became accustomed to the sight and I am ashamed to say that I became indifferent to it. I became inured to the suffering of young men, old men, brothers, sons and fathers, trapped like random prisoners, chained together like horses, heads bent to the ground, leaning forward against the weight, sweat glistening along leathered backs, inching along with no choice but to inch further along and, upon arrival, return to load up once again.

Those who were particularly efficient or enthusiastic would rise in status and were granted authority to help manage the lowest of the low. Not surprisingly, those so rewarded developed intense enthusiasm for the mission. The degree of cruelty they displayed surpassed even that of the project managers. These new evangelists displayed unbound fervor that might have reflected an elevated sense of faith in the mission but, more likely, their brutality was borne of ambition and, perhaps, some vision of freedom. In any event, these minor commanders executed their duties with religious resolve that bordered on fanaticism. They wielded long canes with which to thrash the backs of their former comrades in order to maintain the pace of the work. The whip came down unceasingly and in horrible rhythm: they struck like the hands of the clock of death and the men who bore the brunt of the punishment brandished long scars and open wounds across their backs. The steady drum of the impact of canes upon human skin could be heard across entire sections of the site. It was a common sight to see shirtless men whose torsos were streaked with the crimson grooves of their wounds and their skin oozed red and yellow with infection that never seemed to heal.

Though I was horrified at first, I justified the barbarity in my own mind by the grand nature and purpose of the mission itself. If my enthusiasm for the mission eventually waned, so did my humanity: I simply grew accustomed to these crimes, committed each hour of the day. In fact, if a particular section needed to be cleared in order for me to set lines, I would call for more men to be brought in to remove rock and boulder so that I could complete my work and move on.

There is one incident, however, that I think about with greater frequency as time passes. Some years ago, a member of a work brigade assigned to pull one of the wagons decided one day, for no apparent reason, to refuse to continue. He was not particularly old or infirm; in fact, he seemed as fit as any other member of the labor reserve at that point in time. He simply stopped in his tracks and demanded to be unleashed. The wagon came to a halt; the work could not proceed. One of the project captains noticed the stalled cart and approached. Accompanied by his lieutenant, he walked directly toward the intransigent worker. The captain seemed calm as he drew near. In a casual tone, he ordered the man unchained and separated from his brethren and asked him to step away from the pallet. However, the captain purposely failed to loosen his leg irons. He ordered him to race up an incline toward the crest of a small hill. The man repeatedly tripped and fell as he ran. It was a heartless, humiliating exercise but was only the beginning of his ordeal.

When they arrived at the top of the hill, the captain turned and faced his prisoner. The lieutenant stood directly behind the unfortunate laborer and locked his arm around the man's neck in a manner that barely allowed him to breath. The captive's lips tightened in the form of a grim brown line. He stared at the ground and kept silent and, after the passage of a long agonizing moment, the lieutenant released the man and stepped away. As he did, the rays of the sun highlighted thin red gashes that lined the man's back: fresh wounds from recent whippings. His weathered appearance was due, no doubt, to the course of abuse to which he had been subject but, despite his worn visage, he seemed simple and childlike in voice and demeanor. The captain, on the other hand, exuded the power and cruelty of the soulless desert: his head rose above thick shoulders and his body seemed to have grown out of the ground, an edifice unto himself resembling an ancient dune or hill.

His mustache fell over one side of his lip and he spoke out of the corner of his mouth. "Do we have a problem?" asked the captain. He maintained his cool, detached manner despite the tension of the moment. "No, no . . . no problem," stammered the hapless worker. He grimaced and continued to stare at the ground.

The captain yawned, eyed the worker and then, in a calm yet accusatory tone, addressed his detainee. "But it seems, my friend, that we do have a problem," he said. "The problem, I'm afraid, is you. You are one, just one, among many who have the privilege of working here. Let's keep in mind that we are standing on hallowed ground and, in fact, you've been given the opportunity to participate in a holy undertaking . . . and for whatever ridiculous reason, you have taken it upon yourself to subvert that historic mission. Actually, I don't care what your reason might be. You've decided, quite selfishly, to get in the way and stop the process. It's a problem . . . yes, you are a problem. I'd say that if one, anyone, were to conclude, on any one particular day, that the mission was no longer worthwhile . . . that there was no point to it . . . if he was bored by the work or felt, perhaps like you, that he was too good for it and considered the project to be a waste of his time . . . if he had idiotic thoughts such as these . . ."

The captain paused for a moment, turned his back to his prisoner and slowly walked away, hands clasped behind his back, head bowed as if lost in thought. He then turned back abruptly and faced the simpering worker once again but his tone had changed. He was now furious and his voice reverberated across the dunes. "What would happen if those other decent, dedicated men who stand beside you . . . each one of whom pushes on tirelessly each and every day . . . what if one . . . or some . . . or all . . . what if they entertained the fantasy that they, too, could simply stop . . . stop on a whim . . . and follow the example set by some slacker? They might think, 'well, maybe he's got it right . . . what's the point? Why bother?' And what if all your friends over there . . . ," and at that moment he pointed to the work brigade situated below the hill, still standing, harnessed to the cart. "What if they somehow arrived at the same stupid conclusion and took your lead, decided that they had better things to do, bigger things, greater than the historic mission in which we are now engaged, grander than this crusade . . . our crusade? What if each, that is, what if everyone . . . simply . . . stopped?" he asked. He fell silent and grinned beneath his uneven mustache as if the answer were self-evident. It was a rhetorical question that the wretched worker did not attempt to answer, at least at first. The captain's point had been made and the logic of his argument was unassailable if one accepted, of course, the validity of the premise, i.e., that the excavation of the Garden of Eden was a holy priority, men were at liberty to enslave other men, those so subjugated were duty bound to break their backs in the desert and human lives were expendable.

At this juncture, the doomed man managed to formulate an answer to the question that had been asked though an answer was not expected and certainly not wanted. He looked up but avoided the captain's eyes. "The work can't . . . the work shouldn't stop . . . sir!" he managed to say. His voice was flat and he seemed defeated. His forehead was coated with beads of sweat that reflected the sharp light of the noonday sun. The air was stagnant and there was no sound but for the words that were spoken and the shuffling of feet in the sand.

The remaining members of the work brigade, forced to witness the encounter from the flat path below the hill, waited with apprehension. It was clear to all that this beleaguered man's predicament was dire. Each of them felt relieved that they had been spared the ordeal that he was being forced to endure and each felt guilty for experiencing that sense of relief. They also felt angry and unnerved by the man's weakness and stupidity. They felt resentment, most of all, because the episode was causing them to fall behind schedule and the lost time would have to be made up. They pretended not to notice.

The prisoner's words hung in the air and dissipated in the heat. The project captain didn't bother to respond at that moment but his face swelled and his eyes widened. He appeared as if he were about to explode and words did, in fact, burst from his mouth, loud across the sand so that all could hear him. His words resounded like the words of God that once resonated across the leaves and grasses of Eden long ago: "My word is the law . . . you've known this since day one . . . but you don't care. You chose to disregard me . . . humiliate yourself, disgrace your brothers and undermine the mission. You don't deserve . . . you need to leave . . . get the hell out of here . . . now . . . out of my sight . . . and never come back . . .!"

The stunned worker, paralyzed by fear, couldn't move. He had heard the words but he stood frozen in place. The captain saw that his order had no apparent effect upon his prisoner who, it seemed, was not about to retreat. Again, the captain ordered the man to leave but the traumatized worker was immobilized. "Leave!" yelled the captain but the man, petrified, stood in place. Enraged, the captain grabbed a shovel that lay beside him on the ground, lifted it high in the air with both hands and, in one quick motion, brought it down like a hammer upon the man's head. The laborer slumped to the ground. He lay perfectly motionless. His arms were still coated with the dust of the rubble he had been carting only moments prior. Blood leaked from his forehead. He had collapsed like a boxer who hadn't seen a devastating punch coming. This man, however, was not unconscious like a fallen boxer: this man was dead. The captain signaled for assistance and the corpse was quickly dragged by the feet back down the hill. He was thrown into a ditch adjacent to one of the pits. His body lay there for all to see for quite some time until, in the late afternoon, he was covered. Several workers kicked sand over his carcass and, in a quick moment, he had disappeared. He was gone. The incident never happened, or so it seemed, though it lingered in the hearts of his compatriots and remains fixed in my own memory.

Another man, similar in appearance to the man who had just been killed, was brought in to take his place. It didn't matter that he had a family waiting for him at one of the camps; it didn't matter that he had been lifted out of his life. He was collared and chained and the brigade moved on, this time at a faster pace, pulling the same long, heavy pallet piled high with rock and sand. The new man was strong and, for now, he attacked his work with vigor and focus. He had taken someone else's place but was well aware that, in time, someone else would replace him and he would be left to die. Though he was nameless, blameless and had successfully fallen into step with the platoon of workers who toiled beside him, he was preemptively and presumptively guilty. He was guilty by virtue of who he was. His guilt was an essential aspect of his humanity.

I was not shocked and I was not disturbed. In fact, I was glad to see the dissident laborer removed from the platoon so that the work could proceed. I didn't much care about his fate. The moment he refused to continue, I knew he was as good as gone. I was annoyed, I felt impatient. My job and the general pace of the project was delayed by this minor drama and I had no choice but to work twice as fast to remain caught up with my assignments. Once the man had been dealt with and replaced, my life could continue.

It was not long after this time that I began to have misgivings. My thoughts traveled far beyond the pits and ditches and sand. We had discovered the Garden of Eden, we were within it and we were well into the process of removing it and preserving it. But what, in fact, were we trying to accomplish? How could any of this be justified?

In truth, I had always experienced a deep-seated sense of guilt and I have suffered from this condition for as long as I can recall. It is a disability that has never abated though there is no root cause of which I am aware, no discernable reason and no explicit trigger. It is a state of mind that has always been a part of me and it is, in a sense, a legacy from some place or some time that long preceded me. I am overcome by guilt at every turn and I came to believe that I felt this way simply because I existed. Ultimately, I resigned myself to the permanence of my condition: it seems that I had been lost in it for longer than I could possibly remember, lost in a sea of it, somehow lost before I had consumed my first breath or had taken my first step.

My role in the project only exacerbated this feeling. I came to realize that the entire excavation was itself a grievous, grotesque crime and I had participated in it enthusiastically. I had contributed to a project premised upon the use of human beings as industrial tools. I may not have been a planner and I may have been only a surveyor—but I was complicit. I had been caught up in the spirit of the mission and I had wholeheartedly joined in the venture. No matter how high my level of idealism, no matter the quality of my work, no matter the personal sacrifice I endured toward the realization of a goal that was, ostensibly, laudable and important, the reality was horrific and I was part of it. I was as guilty as any other person involved except, of course, those who had been oppressed by it and beaten into the ground in the course of it.

My sense of guilt flowed through me like a river. It would flood beyond its banks during my conscious hours and the deluge often swept through my dreams at night. I loathed my spiritual being and I detested my physical self as well: I felt my own weight upon the ground, I heard my own footsteps in the shifting sand and I hated each one of them and I hated each moment, hated the feeling of each moment, hated the absence of my own essence and identity. That identity, that core should have been liberated within me long ago and should have shrouded each atom of my being and melded into my spirit but that process had somehow been stunted long ago. I felt the agony of living in the absence of a reason: I felt condemned to live. I worked progressively harder each moment of my life, not to achieve or succeed but, rather, to escape the abscess which was my existence and expunge the guilt that seemed to circulate like blood through the channels of my body. The fact that I had taken part in a mission that was nothing less than a war waged against humanity only contributed to my sense of self-loathing.

I continued to have problems understanding the purpose of the dig and, as time went on, I had trouble coming to terms with it. We had labored to uncover the fabric and spirit of our origin in the hope of embracing it. Even if we had succeeded, nothing would have changed, at least from my perspective. It was silly to think that the excavation of the Garden of Eden would somehow enable us to shed new light upon the past or somehow revitalize history. It was even more absurd to imagine that we could, through our efforts, alter the sequence of events through which we had come into the world. Nothing could undo what had happened long ago: the bite of the apple was a historic reality and that apple could never be made whole again. There is no way to annul the sin and shame implicit in our assumption of deific knowledge, there is no way to alter the reality of our own mortality, there is no way to deny the expulsion from Eden and there is no way for us to purge ourselves of the guilt and trauma that have persisted as part of us since the dawn of our existence. Moreover, there is no way to refute or negate the slaughter we had perpetrated in the desert. We simply cannot ignore the reality of our history and the essence of our nature. Our plight is fixed and continuous: our race toward the past is inexorable as is our descent into a disheartening future. The result of our effort is unalterable no matter how successful we might be in extricating the Garden from the ground and dancing in its ruins.

In any event, despite tragedy and suffering, the work continued at a steady pace. Death at the site became commonplace and there were many casualties. The dying had various causes and took various forms: desert fever, physical injury, exhaustion and execution. These deaths, however, were greatly outnumbered by those that took place at the outlying detention camps where food was scarce, sanitation was inadequate and disease ran rampant. The camps were periodically decimated by outbreaks of cholera. The horror was rendered more horrible through the logistics of death: corpses were dredged away like dead cattle and were cremated in the open air while fresh populations were brought in from outlying regions to replace those who had been lost. In effect, humanity had become a fungible resource and the horrendous level of suffering was overlooked: men, women and children were nothing more than a source of power to sustain a project that would otherwise implode.

◊

By the fifth year, the excavation began to yield impressive results. Every few weeks, a bone, branch or plant was recovered which, after careful analysis, was determined to be authentic. Celebration of these victories propelled the mission further along, especially at times during which enthusiasm seemed to ebb. There came a time, however, at which a truly remarkable development occurred: archeologists believed they had discovered remnants of the Tree of Knowledge. Preliminary reports were encouraging though most of the scientists viewed the evidence as inconclusive. Various studies were initiated but those who had made the discovery were confident that the few bits of bark, calcified fruit and leaves that had drawn their attention would prove to be genuine.

Unfortunately, the reaction at the site was anything but restrained. News of the purported discovery caused a riot. The lowest cadre of workers, lacking hope, a future and any semblance of a life other than one of constant suffering, made a rush for remnants of the Tree that had been carefully set aside. It was a pitiful scene: the workers, after having managed to loosen their chains, ran as one from the staging area like some manic herd. They were frantic and charged from one corner of the site to the other in a desperate search for vestiges of the Tree. Once they had stumbled upon the cases that housed the sacred remains, the herd broke apart and each man fought off the other in a frenzied attempt to break open containers and grab as many pieces as possible. They believed these sticks and twigs had been sanctified by God and could somehow empower them to overcome their overseers and break the bonds of their imprisonment. Those who carried off tree fragments proceeded to eat what they had grabbed in the belief that they could thereby acquire some modicum of divine knowledge and power in order to liberate themselves. They soon fell sick though they did recover after a short while. The unfortunate truth was that the bits they had consumed were random remains that had no connection with the Garden of Eden. The scientists had been wrong.

Chaos prevailed in the hours that followed until the rioters were overcome by their overseers. Eight men were killed in the course of the rebellion. *So this, I suppose, is Eden,* I thought to myself, *the new Eden, the real Eden.* I watched in horror as the men fought and gradually exhausted themselves as cadres of guards quickly surrounded them and gained control. The guards bound the men in chain, pummeled them with canes and forced them to stand and bear witness to one execution after another. These men were criminals: they had violated the law and they were no longer innocent. Order had to be preserved and the law required that these men be expelled from the human nation. This was the truth of the desert, miles from the world, miles from the heart of civilization, long after the Garden of Eden had died and had sunk into the ground.

The minor rebellion that took place that day was quickly suppressed. There were other rebellions from time to time which were all quashed in the same summary fashion. The torture continued, the killing continued and, despite the abject inhumanity of the project, the work continued. However, the project was beset by additional problems that, collectively, had a corrosive effect upon unity. These issues were endemic and intractable: frequent disruption of communications, equipment failure, shortages of spare parts, cost overruns and security concerns were but a few of the myriad logistical challenges that plagued the project. Responses and solutions were typically hampered by incompetence and delay caused by labyrinthine bureaucratic procedures. Moreover, planning was erratic and strategies varied with each incoming political administration. Though these difficulties were consequential, I believe these problems were exacerbated by the immense stress and frustration experienced by top tier managers and planners. They were, as a group, suspicious, territorial and quick to oppose each other at every turn. In essence, the leadership came to wage war upon itself. For these reasons, progress slowed as time went on. The project seemed interminable.

The greatest practical problem to emerge, however, was confusion over the goal of the project itself. The objectives of the mission had shifted over time and, at this juncture, it was difficult to find agreement as to its ultimate purpose. It was also questionable whether the mission, however defined, was still achievable. Those who were "realist" in their approach had concluded that the project was no longer viable. They believed that the project had served to stratify society rather than unify it. In their view, the mission had become unmanageable and constituted an unacceptable drain upon available resources. They petitioned for an end to the project and proposed that remnants extracted thus far be placed on exhibit but the remainder of the Garden be left in the ground and reburied.

There was also a religious contingent whose members had formerly been fiercely in favor of the project but now demanded that the project come to an immediate halt. The collection of remnants that had been retrieved thus far was so prosaic and unremarkable in their eyes as to cause a panic among them. Their fear was that religious faith and the holy word, established through thousands of years of worship and commitment, would be degraded, impugned or even contradicted were the Garden to be wholly extracted and systematically examined. Proponents of this position insisted that the Garden be reburied and the site be permanently sealed. They also demanded that all remains recovered thus far be destroyed.

There were those, of course, who wished to continue to the end. The glory of the mission no longer shone brightly in their minds. They maintained, however, that it would be catastrophic to cease our efforts at this juncture, especially after so much time, money and effort had been invested in the project. This group, perhaps the smallest but most ardent, had convinced themselves that the problems we experienced were strictly logistical and could be overcome, in time, through innovation, creative thinking and reliance upon emerging technology. In short, they believed it was too late in the game to stop. To terminate at this point would constitute an admission that the entire project was a mistake. The implication would be calamitous: social order would rupture and society would descend into chaos.

These differences could not be resolved. Difficulties proliferated and disharmony reached greater, more profound levels as time went on. The most controversial aspect of the project—the issue of forced labor—was continuously debated but a resolution was never realized. It became clear, as the dispute dragged on, that the labor issue was irreconcilable and, ultimately, the problem was simply disregarded.

Perhaps the saddest truth and greatest failing of the project arose out of an inherent contradiction rooted in the mission as originally conceived. The vastness of the undertaking and immense breadth of vision that gave rise to it was, in fact, the cause of its demise. One generation confidently handed off the work to the next with the expectation that the work would continue with unabated resolve but, through the course of each transfer, the inspiration that initially gave impetus to the mission faded a bit further. By the time I retired, it was rare that the young planners and managers who had been brought in to continue the mission had any familiarity with the story of the Garden. Each generation of specialists who helped bring the Garden to the surface were less aware than their predecessors of the unique significance and critical position the Garden held in our history. As time went on, a dwindling number of those involved in the undertaking had any sense of it. Though it had survived the passage of millennia, the meaning of the Garden was lost in the sand of the desert. The work proceeded through the force of its own inertia but the point of the project was missing.

This spiritual erosion was aggravated by the way in which the work was carried out. The project had been carefully broken down into a series of stages, each of which required the completion of plans, tasks and jobs within fixed time frames as measured and understood in familiar, human terms, in keeping with clock and calendar. Our notion of time, however, was inadequate as a basis to comprehend the Garden as a whole. The Garden seemed to stand outside the boundaries of time as we understood and experienced it, perhaps quite different than the way time was experienced by others ages ago. It is even questionable whether time as we know it even existed during the Garden of Eden epoch. We simply weren't capable of embracing the Garden in a way that transcended time as a construct other than as one fragmented and arranged into groupings of days, weeks and hours. A comprehensive work schedule was illusory at best because the project, like some overwhelming monolith, could not be wholly understood by any one person or completed within a single lifetime. It was as if we stood within the shadow of a huge skyscraper that we knew to be immensely tall but were too close to its walls to see the top. Consequently, the mission drained into the crevices that ran between the thousands of moments that comprised it. Understandably, the division of the grand scheme into sub-projects, carried out in accordance with the dictates of a day planner, was the only methodology available in order for us to grapple with so immense an undertaking: we are, after all, only human. Nevertheless, the division of the work into timebound stages and sub-projects served to undermine the grand scheme itself.

Moreover, the division of labor between various groups of managers, specialists and workers, a standard feature of any modern industrial enterprise, actually contributed to the disfunction and impeded progress. Myriad managers and laborers whose responsibility it was to complete specified jobs were scattered among operations teams that constantly gained and lost personnel through the typical course of promotion, transfer and attrition. Thus, the character of the work force changed continuously and, over time, it was the case that sundry work teams weren't even aware of the existence of other teams engaged in the same general effort or endeavor. And though it is true that many of the technicians were highly advanced in a particular science or discipline, the most gifted among them lacked the capacity to understand, in any meaningful way, the work of colleagues who had different issues upon which to focus. They may have worked at desks within a few steps of each other but, in a real sense, each technician's work was so specialized that it was impossible for any one person to absorb more than a tiny fragment of the project as a whole. These technicians, characteristic of the entire workforce, were afflicted with a professional myopia dictated by the limitations of his or her education, experience, the inviolable set of requirements and expectations determined by managers and the utter enormity and shifting scope of the mission itself.

For this reason, the very people who were charged with the success of the project were incapable of understanding its scope and significance. Completion of disparate jobs that had no inherent meaning in themselves became, in the final analysis, the sole and ultimate goal of the mission. It might be more accurate to say that the mission no longer existed as originally conceived but had devolved into a thousand minor missions loosely connected within the netting of a nebulous plan.

Despite these realities, the project continues to be funded, even at this late date. The work has become a norm of existence and, like the scenery one routinely passes on his way home, it is an aspect of everyday life to which we have become oblivious. It is also a burden that grows heavy over the course of time. Given the impasse that has arisen as to its future, it seems likely that the work will continue indefinitely. Despite the many problems, the truth is that the excavation has become a raison d'être: it is the heartbeat of contemporary society. No one believes that the project can or will end in his or her own lifetime and no one speaks of the day upon which the work will be finished. The prospect of completion seems utterly frightening: once the work is done, what would be left? What project could possibly be meaningful once the source of all meaning has been unearthed and placed on display? No one dares to imagine how many generations of work and sacrifice will pass before the excavation is deemed "complete."

My retirement as a surveyor was, in actuality, a dismissal and was not at all voluntary. I was perceived as too old, at this point, to discharge my duties effectively and I was suspect in the eyes of incoming managers who had new ideas as to the meaning, purpose and direction of the mission. I was thought to be an impediment simply because I was so very aware of the history of the project: I knew how it had come into being and I knew how it had meandered in purpose and scope. I was the repository of institutional memory that no one wanted to remember.

Since my dismissal, I have heard that much of my work has been revised or discarded as new minds see the land differently, new instruments are relied upon and advanced technologies are developed but, in my view, the ongoing survey work seems redundant and, for that reason, a bit senseless. Nevertheless, for what it's worth, I compare boundary lines of the Garden that I had drawn when I first arrived with those set forth on recent surveys that I've managed to acquire. I am pleased, to a certain extent, to see that my calculations were not too far off though it doesn't much matter in the scheme of things: it is inevitable that technology yet to be developed will render even the newest surveys obsolete and inaccurate.

I was kept on, however, to run the small museum recently established to conserve and display ancient remains and document the history of the project. It is a small building that sits upon ground that I once surveyed long ago. There are few visitors and I sit at the front desk with much time to myself. Housed within various glass cases and cabinets are fossilized bits of wood, leaves, ancient seed and a variety of other remains. On occasion, an old surveyor or scientist will come through to review some of the old records. We are also visited, from time to time, by former administrators who seek to come to terms with their own role in the undertaking. Members of the clergy often retreat to the museum to bask in the cool air that circulates within our exhibition rooms and, every few months, we receive groups of school children who are driven out all this way to study the Garden. They hardly glance at the collection of twigs and vines that are neatly labeled beneath thick glass: clearly, they are bored by the exercise. I watch as they lean on those cabinets, their elbows steeped in the dust that has swept in from the desert, accumulated over the course of years.

The excavation continues. Miserable souls continue to be conscripted into labor brigades and are forced to pull the same old, creaking wagons and pallets. Men continue to dig, anthropologists continue to sift through all that has been lifted out of the ground and administrators continue to push the project to its inglorious end, whenever that may come. Running the museum is the best I could hope for at this point and is, in truth, quite enough for me to handle.

I am unaware of any recent discoveries or grand projects that have stimulated public attention. If the tablets of Moses were to be discovered beneath the ground at the foot of some mountain or if the branches of the burning bush were to be uncovered within the heart of a sand dune in the desert, I'm sure such discovery would generate a new sense of excitement and give rise to new projects and new realities. At this juncture, all that is beyond my ability to comprehend and, certainly, I would not have the energy or will to play any part in it.

At the Beach

Stand upon the gravel sand
At the ocean's edge,
Crusted lip where the sand crabs live.

Soft water ripples:
They flee from the sea
And roll for miles,
Die at your feet,
Seep through the sand
Without a whisper,
Barely a hint of the eternal war
That rages so far away;
Swollen waves:
They rise, implode,
Crash and die
Beneath a foam white coverlet
That looms like smoke
Above a matte green fire;
As old as age, the grand disorder.

The sun and planets turn away,
The moon pretends it cannot see;
Water ripples at your feet:
The apocalyptic aftermath,
Apocalypse that never ends.

Beyond

Beside the ancient ocean,
Beyond the final star,
No light, no sound
No remonstration
But for the rhythm
Of your breathing,
Resists the frigid air.

Nothing to be done
But brace against the cutting wind;
It skips across the surf,
Sees you standing
On the shore;
It drives like mad
To meet you there.

Assateague

I want to go to Assateague
And watch wild horses ride;
Speckled grey, mottled black,
Skin worn thin like linen flesh
Hanging on the line,
Stained and bruised;
They wear their wounds like epaulettes,
Their scars like battle ribbons
And in their rage, they run,
They fight, they kick and bite;
They rip each other's hide apart
And bleed upon the ground;
They trip and fall and scream,
And slide across the mud;
They flail about and when they fall
They break their bones
Beneath the weight of who they are;
They levy war but don't know why
And when the peace of death prevails
The scores they had in mind
Remain unsettled as before.

The fallen are forgotten,
Left to lie in sand and weed;
Their squeals are frightening to the dying
And as they die, they mourn;
They sing of death's ignominy;
They close their eyes,
Their skins grow dry:
They lie beneath the carcasses
Of other horses, dead or dying;
Their lungs collapse, their breathing stops:
So ends the trauma of their dying.

The horses that survive
Run headlong upon the beach;
They race along the waterline
And cool their hooves in shallow pools,
Exultant and alive;
Flaring nostrils, insane eyes,
They scream ecstatic, arrogant and satisfied;
They taunt the dead and strut as if exempt
From laws that govern living things;
They crush the shells that line the beach
Beneath their bloody feet;
They mark the sand in red
And claim it as their own;
They breathe long draughts
Of fetid air as blood and myth and mania
Resound within their consciousness;
Tidal waters recede as quickly as they came,
Chastened by the butchery,
Sickened by the slaughter
As darkness drops like stone
And horses sing in praise of Death
And worship at its alter.

The horses that run at Assateague
Don't speak or think or speculate;
Never do they hide from death
But live or die upon the beach
And if they live, they run once more;
Those horses have no rider:
Death decides the race;
Their truth is raw and unadorned
And I must watch them ride.

The New Windhover

Obsidian eyes,
Hard hook beak,
Stiff black feathers
Stretched like fingers,
Legs like stems
Like knotted wood
And shoulders curved;
Wings like arms but tapered thin,
Sharp stiletto arrow tips;
He rises through the atmosphere,
Hovers high above the earth,
Bathes in freezing breeze
Rushing past his ears and eyes;
He hears the lonesome drone of air
And sings as he ascends.

His claws, however, understand
That the edifice cannot survive
Unless it eats; hunger throbs within his feet
And they long to kill so the whole may live;
They see with innate eyes
The shadow of death that looms below
And races along in unison;
Like anchors hanging from the bow,
They weigh it down;
The hulk descends to earth
And hunts above the cotton grass.

Thus, the unremitting tension
Embedded in its being:
One must fly both high and low,
An inherent contradiction that is,
At once, its legacy and fate
And, in time, will rip the whole apart.

I saw him descend upon a field
And then rise up again,
His variable trajectory
Quite unlike the hawk
That hovered so majestically
In Hopkins' mind but flew away
(And won't return, presumably);
An obscure metaphor
That lingers in air;
A prayer from an age gone by
Embedded in a poem;
It drifts along an ebbing tide
In which poets' ghosts drown;
No headstones upon that sorry sea,
Little to demark the faith and dreams
Of disremembered generations;
Holy dappled agent of God
Stilled above the earth:
Its beauty was transformative
Or so we were told so long ago.

What I May Become

I wish I had my captain's hat. I can't find it. I have never been a captain and I don't really want to be a captain but it's gone. I need to find it. I am quite lost without it.

My captain's hat is no ordinary hat. It is exceptional though standard to some degree: it has a cloud-white crown, flexible enough to billow with air when worn but strong enough to maintain its form against the assault of winter winds. Its cloth top sits upon a stiff headband which, in turn, is seated firmly within a black circular collar. It never loses the circle of its obsessive crease. It has a narrow black bill slanted at an angle in the traditional way, reflective like patent leather, practically blinding when the sun sits high against the sky and the whole assemblage fits upon my head as if it were meant to be. A thick gold cloth braid stretches across the front, tight against it, just above the top edge of the bill for all to see. It is neatly knotted at each end and these knots are so important because they provide a sense of resolve and form and balance that I can't otherwise seem to find within myself. Emblazoned upon the bill are four gold leaves, two identical sets at each end etched in uncompromising yellow thread, stiff upon the brim, and each set is pointed toward the other in perfect, perpetual tension. Without the braid and gold leaves, my captain's hat would seem less significant, less regal and less imposing than at present in which case I would feel considerably less situated in the world and hardly connected to it.

Mounted to the front of the cloud-white crown, facing directly out and apparent to the world like a centerpiece, is a small dark square patch. There is no insignia, anchor, crest or eagle etched thereon but there is, rather, a detailed depiction of an ancient skeleton emblazoned upon it for all to see: an archetypal human skeleton, a

143

glorious skeleton set forth in full and proportionate height and breadth. The emblem of the skeleton is meticulously sewn into the cloth in tight gold stitching. It is bright like a headlight and, if one looks carefully, one would notice that the skeleton is portrayed as if it is in motion. There is little doubt that this skeleton figure is engaged in some variety of dance, unworldly to a degree. The bones of his body are bright and dominant against the black night background of the patch. His jig is daring and unencumbered and free and he is fully committed, uninhibited, euphoric and unbridled and all this is revealed in the neatly embroidered image posted within the borders of that small dark badge. No one who encounters me can avoid it or ignore it, even at a distance. It is as if this small emblem announces my presence and explains the nature of my character. The skeleton holds his right arm above his head and points to the sky. You can see the tip of his forefinger which he holds high overhead. His left leg is bent at an awkward angle. He is smiling, continually smiling, and I've often felt that smile to be somewhat seductive yet malicious and intimidating in some odd way. All this is stitched within the small space of that simple, dull cloth backdrop that is forever sealed to the front of a hat that fits so perfectly atop my head.

Now, after having contemplated my hat for these few moments, I realize, once again, that it is gone and I begin to feel the familiar nausea of disappointment and anxiety and fear course within me much like the rise and fall of the sea and the rolling of its swells. As has occurred so many times before, I feel that sickness surge through the very inlets and channels and rivulets interspersed within the deepest regions of my psyche. I know, at this point in my life, that it is an anomalous procession of hopelessness that staggers through me like some jazz funeral parade that lurches chaotically forward, left and right, as it ushers the deceased and mourners to the grave. It stumbles through the middle of me, time and again, with increasing frequency and you could say, at this juncture, that this sickness has become a fairly constant companion. And it is true that, over the course of time, I have become increasingly lost within myself and my bewilderment is more than disconcerting and disturbing though I do my best, nonetheless, to go about the business of my life. I am afraid, I am tired and, at this critical moment, I cannot find the only thing that grounds, comforts and connects me to the world and this disjunction between myself and the world is frightening. It has been my hat, in the last analysis, that has served as the one thing, the very thing, the only thing that has allowed my inner self to speak. You can't understand it unless you live it and I have a profound fear that the loss of my hat will be the end of me. For this reason, after giving the matter much thought, I have made the decision to become a skeleton, I shall be my own skeleton. I shall starve myself so that I may thereby transform myself and become the thing that is the quintessence of what I have lost and, through such transformation, I shall find myself. I shall rediscover myself in a way that is greater and grander and more rewarding than ever. Heretofore, a skeleton was but an image appended to the front of a hat that I posted like a signpost atop my head. I will make a change: from this moment on, I will no longer express my nature through a symbol that, I now realize, has served, thus far, as more of a prop than a manifestation of my true self. Instead, I shall embody, truly and completely, the person that, formerly, I could only express as an abstraction. I shall become the genuine articulation of my own body, soul and spirit and I shall manifest myself in a meaningful way, a direct way even though my particular form of self-expression may overawe or chill the spirit or unsettle the mind of those who cross my path. In any event, they will know precisely who I am. I shall become, simply, the most austere and clear form of myself that is within my power to be. And when the flesh of me has melted away, I shall consist of bones only and those bones shall yellow with age and dry in time and shall be rough about the edges and I shall arrange myself in postures and stances that reflect the true and only self that wells up within me in a way that, admittedly, I am hardly able to fathom or

145

comprehend at present. In time, on a day that will someday arrive, soon or long from now, I will know, without doubt, that I have achieved the proper expression of skeletonship and will have become the true and only reflection of the person I really am. On that day, I shall raise my arm to the heavens and beckon and gesture in the same manner as the skeleton that adorned the hat that I once wore, now forever lost. I shall point to the sky and I shall step in odd, devastating rhythm and I shall dance the dance of death. I shall look at you intently through the hollow holes of my eyes and you shall know that I have summoned you and you shall become my brother in arms or my sister in mourning and you shall see me and you shall come to know the very core of me.

I Come and Go

in a dream
she summoned me,
death shroud night gown
kept her warm;
sunken shoulders,
light beige cloth.

I saw her march
through desert night,
carbon black
like Rembrandt's hat,
darker than the ceiling
you know is there
but cannot find
when roused from sleep
by troubled thoughts
disguised as dreams.

she stepped upon the sand
as if it were a street;
no mission, no considered route;
she meandered, yes, she wandered,
among the dunes, she wore no shoes,
those tiny grains of sand were sharp,
they cut her tired feet.

I heard her call
from the edge of a dream;
I turned my gaze
to the blood-soaked sand;
she wasn't alone:
a parade of mourners
followed her,
legions dressed
in tattered rags,

consumed with grief;
footsteps sinking into sand,
they stepped
and then they stepped again,
relentless, undeterred,
headlong into frigid air.

(I was among them
long ago
but took my leave
in deference
to that trifling embryo
of hope that twisted
in its sleep,
hidden in some
part of me.)

that night
so dark,
that night
grew darker,
it fell upon the ground;
I heard the sum
of suffering,
the long eternal groan;
I heard the night
explode
and blackness
seeped into the sand
like rain, and overflowed,
concealed the earth,
diffused the air,
obscured my view
of the long parade
that staggered toward oblivion;

I looked out but could only see
an outline of the up and down
of arms and legs
and curvature of bodies
moving back and forth,
vague and imprecise,
all but lost to me
in the catacomb that was
the darkest of all nights,
and though I could barely see
those pilgrims pass in front of me,
I could hear them perfectly;
I heard them chant
in the ancient way,
a messianic song,
modal formulation,
chimes like holy carillons:
their voices rose in air,
fell like tears upon the dunes
and drained within the fabric
of the dream I had that night.

in time, they were gone
and when the last
had disappeared,
I woke up, I lay awake,
safe within the ancient woods,
unbound and unconstrained
for no apparent reason,
and at that moment
I understood that I was free;
I reveled in my sense of self,
alive and unafraid,
and peace flowed into me;
I rested on the forest floor;

I didn't want a thing
and nothing wanted me;
I released the dream I had
and it abandoned me.

I saw the dawn descend,
it looked for me,
it came to me,
it sifted
settled
came to rest
upon the grass
like a sheet unfurled
that slowly floats
and falls upon a bed
and in the light of that one day,
the world revealed itself to me:
yellow petaled flowers
shrugged lazy in the air,
squirrels engaged
in stutter race
between the roots of trees;
a soft breeze lifted leaves
and let them fall again
and I stood up
and breathed the air.

that human chain
was forever gone;
only I remained
and I was free:
one person,
a singularity
of my own design,

my soul a monument
to that part of me
that wouldn't die
but resolved to wait
for the advent of day
which did, in fact, arrive
and, on that day, I was released,
salvaged from a dream I had,
perfectly alive in the world
on the first of mornings yet to come:
the light was crystalline;
I danced upon the earth;
I jumped and ran;
I shook my arms and hands;
I leaped in directions
I never knew were there;
I stamped my feet upon the ground;
I lifted my eyes to see beyond
the acquiescent sky;
I saw an iridescent light
and felt its warm embrace.

the world was awake
and, in that waking hour,
the earth was resonant
with tympanic pulse
of beating hearts,
and all those living things
conspired in collective riot:
trees threw back their branches,
wriggled out from stations
in which they had been planted
so very long ago,

frozen in earth
since time began,
now were free;
liberated, they ran rampant,
they danced in front of me;
I heard them sing
and I began to sing as well,
a song the ancients
dared not sing:
a song of death's demise
leaped from my lungs
and out my mouth,
loud and clear,
in perfect pitch and tone,
a song as buoyant
as life itself;
it shook the leaves,
echoed in the ground,
resounded in the dirt and rock
and rang within the depths
in which the polities
of space and time
had been interred
so long ago.

I sang for myself
and whoever else
could hear my voice:
I sang for those who cannot sing,
for those who cannot see,
for those who walk forever
in circles that don't close,
for those who stand
in long, suffering line,
for those who die alone,

and for the diaspora
of lost and scattered souls
who wander through the night.

I sang and I shall sing again,
to the ends of the universe
until those ends are one, once more
and are bound in time,
in a place beyond
the singed night's edge,
deep within the dawn
that stretches young arms,
smooth and strong, and yawns,
and lifts its head and opens eyes
as wide and open as the sky:
they are the doors
through which I wander, walk, I run,
I come and go . . .

About the Author

Walter Weinschenk is an attorney, writer, and musician. Until a few years ago, he wrote short stories exclusively but now divides his time equally between poetry and prose. Walter's writing has appeared in a number of literary publications including *The Carolina Quarterly, Lunch Ticket, Cathexis Northwest Press, Meniscus Literary Journal, The Banyan Review,* and *Sand Hills Literary Magazine.* Walter lives in a suburb just outside Washington, D.C. More of Walter's writing can be found at walterweinschenk.com.